Quiz Book

Astronomy

1000+ Amazing questions kids must know

Dr. R.K. Sharma

Universe	Galaxies	Stars	Constellations	Sun	Planets	Dwarf Planets
Moons	Solar Eclipse	Lunar eclipse	Asteroids	Meteors	Comets
Picture Quiz	Mixed Quiz	Puzzles

Copyright © 2020 Dr RK Sharma

All rights reserved No part of this book may be reproduced, or stored in a retrieval system, or transmitted in any form or by any means, electronic, mechanical, photocopying, recording, or otherwise, without express written permission of the publisher.

Table of Contents

1. Introduction... 7

2. About the Author 8

3. The Universe 9

    Quiz-1 10

    Quiz-2 13

4. Galaxies... 16

    Quiz-3 17

5. The Milky Way Galaxy 20

    Quiz-4 21

6. Stars.. 24

    Quiz-5 25

    Quiz-6 28

7. Constellations 35

    Quiz-7 36

    Quiz-8 39

    Quiz-9 42

8. The Sun 52

    Quiz-10.. 53

    Quiz-11 56

9. Mercury... 59

    Quiz-12.. 60

10. Venus 63

    Quiz-13.. 64

11. The Earth... 67

    11.1 The Planet Earth 68

    Quiz-14.. 68

    Quiz-15.. 71

11.2 The Interior of the Earth 74

Quiz-16 74

11.3 Geographical Features of Earth 77

Quiz-17 77

11.4 Seasons on Earth 80

Quiz-18 80

Quiz-19 83

11.5 The Earth's Atmosphere 86

Quiz-20 86

12. Mars 89

Quiz-21 90

13. Jupiter 93

Quiz-22 94

14. Saturn 97

Quiz-23 98

15. Uranus 101

Quiz-24 102

16. Neptune 105

Quiz-25 106

17. The Earth's Moon 109

17.1 The Earth's Moon 110

Quiz-26 110

Quiz-27 113

17.2 Phases of the Moon 116

Quiz-28 116

17.3 The Moon Mission 120

Quiz-29 120

Quiz-30 123

18. Other Moons of Solar System..126

    Quiz-31...127

19. Dwarf Planets 130

    Quiz-32...131

20. Solar Eclipse 134

    Quiz-33...135

21. Lunar Eclipse 138

    Quiz-34...139

22. Asteroids & Meteorites 143

    Quiz-35...144

23. Comets..147

    Quiz-36...148

24. Solar System-Mixed Quiz 151

    Quiz-37...152

    Quiz-38...155

    Quiz-39...158

    Quiz-40...161

    Quiz-41...164

    Quiz-42...167

    Quiz-43...177

25. Your weight & Age on Planets 184

    Quiz-44...185

26. Famous Astronomers 188

    Quiz-45...189

    Quiz-46...192

27. Crossword Puzzle in Astronomy 195

Quiz-47..195

Quiz-48..196

28. Search the word Puzzle in Astronomy 197

Quiz-49..197

29. Unscramble the letters in Astronomy..................................198

Quiz-50..198

Quiz-51..199

30. Answers to all quizzes 200

31. Disclaimer 217

1. Introduction

We all are fascinated as well as perplexed by our unimaginably vast Universe and the mysteries surrounding it. Our Universe comprises of trillions of stars, galaxies, black holes, enormous clouds of gases, and many other fascinating objects in the Universe. Right from our childhood, we have been curious to unwind the mysteries of the Universe and the following questions always came to our mind:

- How did the Universe evolve? How vast is the Universe?
- What are galaxies and stars? What are constellations?
- What is the solar system? What are planets, moons, asteroids, meteorites, dwarf planets, comets?
- What are solar & lunar eclipses; How moon keeps changing its shape?
- What is your weight & age on different planets?
- How did mankind land on the Moon?
- Who are the pioneers in astronomy?
- And the list goes on....

This interesting Quiz Book on Astronomy for kids answers the above questions by bringing out well-planned quizzes on a variety of topics in Multiple Choice Question format. This exciting quiz book is the perfect learning and entertainment tool for kids of all ages, aspirants to various competitive examinations, and quiz buffs.

This fun-filled quiz book takes you on a journey to the mysterious world of the Universe, galaxies, stars, constellations, solar system, planets, asteroids, comets, etc. Additional quizzes on Moon exploration, solar & lunar eclipses, phases of moons, picture quizzes, comparison of planets, weight & age on different planets, pioneers of astronomy, puzzles, jumbled word, search the word etc. are also given. The answers to all the questions are also given.

So, enjoy your journey to the mysteries of the Universe!

(Dr Rakesh Kumar Sharma)
e-mail: rks.aesi@gmail.com

2. About the Author

The author of this quiz book, Dr. Rakesh Kumar Sharma is a Ph.D. in Aerospace Engineering from the Indian Institute of Science, Bangalore, India. He served as a Scientist in the Government of India and Professor in Aerospace Department, India. He has authored/co-authored many books on Aerospace subjects.

He has special interest in writing Science Series books for Kids

3. The Universe

Quiz-1

1. Which theory explains the evolution of the Universe?

   A. Supernova   B. Big bang

   C. Kepler's Theory   D. Blackhole

2. Which is the largest star in the universe?

   A. Sun   B. Sirius

   C. Pole Star   D. UY Scuti

3. Which is the largest known galaxy in the universe?

   A. Whirlpool   B. IC 1101

   C. Andromeda   D. Milky Way

4. Heavy stars go through --- before turning into black holes

   A. Supernova   B. Big Bang

   C. Celestial event   D. None of the above

5. What do we mean by Nebula?

   A. The great explosion in space

   B. Asteroid belt

   C. A cloud of gas and dust in outer space.

   D. Meteorites entering earth

6. The universe is constantly expanding making it impossible to reach the edge

   A. True

   B. False

7. Which astronomer placed Earth at the centre of the universe?

A. Claudius Ptolemy
B. Galileo Galilei
C. Tycho Brahe
D. Aryabhata

8. Which astronomer suggested that the Sun was at the centre of the solar system?

A. Nicolaus Copernicus
B. Hypatia
C. Claudius Ptolemy
D. Tycho Brahe

9. Who was the first astronomer to use a telescope?

A. Leonardo da Vinci
B. Galileo Galilei
C. Claudius Ptolemy
D. Hypatia

10. What is a light year?

A. Distance between the Sun and the Earth
B. Distance travelled by light in one year
C. Angstrom Unit (AU)
D. Unit of time

11. Heliocentric means around ----

A. The Sun
B. The Moon
C. Jupiter
D. Neptune

12. The study of the origin and evolution of the universe is known as

A. Tomography
B. Cystoscopy
C. Cryptology
D. Cosmology

13. According to Kepler's Laws, the cube of the mean distance of a planet from the sun is proportional to the ---

A. Swept out area
B. Square of the period
C. Cube of the period
D. Square root of period

14. A blackhole with the mass of the earth would be the size of
   A. The Sun
   B. The Moon
   C. A Marble
   D. A hot air balloon

15. The reason we call an astronomical body a black hole is that
   A. It is a huge star which appears black at its centre.
   B. Its gravity is so high that it absorbs its own photons.
   C. It represents lack of matter in a portion of space.
   D. It is a dead planet.

16. In which year, the Hubble Telescope was launched into space?
   A. 1985
   B. 1990
   C. 1995
   D. 2000

17. The position in the sky directly overhead is called?
   A. Azimuth
   B. Attitude
   C. Zenith
   D. Ecliptic

18. What is the approximate age of the Universe?
   A. 14 thousand years
   B. 14 million years
   C. 14 billion years
   D. None of the above

19. The Hubble Space Telescope is named after which American astronomer
   A. Mark Hubble
   B. Aldrin Hubble
   C. Edwin Hubble
   D. None of the above

20. The distance from the center of the sun to the center of the earth is called?
   A. One Parsec
   B. One Light year
   C. One Astronomical Unit
   D. None of the above

Quiz-2

1. A light-year is a unit for measuring ----
   A. Time   B. Distance
   C. Solar Radiations   D. Speed

2. Parsec is a basic unit of length for measuring distances to stars and galaxies. One Parsec is equal to ----
   A. 1 light year   B. 2.45 light years
   C. 3.26 light years   D. 6.8 light years

3. The instrument used to observe the stars and determine their position on the Horizon
   A. Telescope   B. Altimeter
   C. Sundial   D. Astrolabe

4. What instrument is used for measuring the angular altitude of a star above the Horizon?
   A. Astrolabe   B. Telescope
   C. Sextant   D. Sundial

5. As per Aristotle's proposed model of the solar system, what was at the center?
   A. Earth   B. Sun
   C. Moon   D. Saturn

6. The prefix helio means...?
   A. Estrella   B. Luna
   C. Tierra   D. Sol

7. What is the average distance from the center of the earth to the center of the Sun?
   A. 1 AU   B. 2 AU
   C. 4 AU   D. 10 AU

8. Copernicus proposed a model to explain planetary motion. His model was called ...

   A. Geocentric model   B. Heliocentric model

   C. Electric model   D. Kepler's model

9. Who first proposed the theory of Big-Bang in 1927?

   A. Galileo Galilei   B. Georges Lemaitre

   C. Copernicus   D. Stephen Hawking

10. Which of the following is the correct statement about the blackhole?

   A. Nobody can see a black hole

   B. It has extremely strong gravity

   C. These are extremely compact space objects

   D. All of the above

11. Which spacecraft was used to lift-off the famous Hubble telescope?

   A. Discovery   B. Challenger

   C. Endeavor   D. Soyuz 2

12. At what altitude the Hubble Telescope orbits the Earth?

   A. 252 km   B. 386 km

   C. 462 km   D. 560 km

13. Most of the mass in the Universe appears to exist in an unknown form called?

   A. Blackhole   B. Dark matter

   C. Dense core   D. None of the above

14. As per astronomical measurements, the distant galaxies are

   A. Approaching each other   B. Moving in circles

   C. Stationary   D. Moving apart

15. What is the meaning of redshift?

A. The collapsing of a star
B. The Universe is expanding

C. A highly luminous radiation.
D. Shifting of Sun's red spots

16. One parsec is the distance at the Sun that spans ---

A. 1 sec of arc
B. 1 minute of arc

C. 1 hour of arc
D. 3600 hours of arc

17. 1 light year =

A. 9.46×10^8 km
B. 9.46×10^{10} km

C. 9.46×10^{12} km
D. 9.46×10^{14} km

18. The telescope was invented by ---

A. Hans Lippershey
B. Nicolas Copernicus

C. John Kepler
D. Galileo

19. 1 parsec =

A. 1 light years
B. 3.26 light years

C. 4.84 light years
D. 10 light years

20. How many billion kilometers are there in 1AU?

A. 1
B. 25

C. 100
D. 150

4. Galaxies

Quiz-3

1. Approximately how many galaxies are there in the universe?

   A. 50 billion
   B. 100 billion
   C. 200 billion
   D. 200 trillion

2. A huge collection of gas, dust, and stars and their solar systems is called ---

   A. Star
   B. Galaxy
   C. Asteroid
   D. Comet

3. How many stars are there in the Milky Way galaxy?

   A. 100 million
   B. 400 million
   C. 400 billion
   D. 400 trillion

4. We live in which galaxy?

   A. The Milky Way galaxy
   B. Andromeda galaxy
   C. IC 1101
   D. Cigar galaxy

5. Astronomers believe that our Milky Way galaxy will someday collide with --- galaxy

   A. Andromeda
   B. Bode's
   B. Comet
   D. IC 1101

6. Our Milky Way galaxy is what type of galaxy?

   A. Irregular
   B. Elliptical
   C. Circular
   D. Spiral

7. Which galaxy has arms and a central bulge?

   A. An elliptical galaxy
   B. An arm galaxy
   C. A spiral galaxy
   D. An irregular galaxy

8. Which type of galaxy is the largest?

   A. Spiral   B. Elliptical

   C. Circular   D. Irregular

9. Which is the largest known galaxy in the universe?

   A. Whirlpool   B. IC 1101

   C. Andromeda   D. Milky Way

10. How many light-years across is the Milky Way?

    A. 1,000   B. 10,000

    C. 100,000   D. 1000,000

11. Which is the closest galaxy to Earth outside the Milky Way?

    A. Sombrero   B. Andromeda

    C. Antennae   D. NGC 2770

12. The galaxies are categorized by

    A. Number of stars   B. Shape

    C. Size   D. Colour

13. In most of the galaxies, what is found at its center?

    A. A giant blackhole   B. Giant Sun

    C. A big bang   D. A small Sun

14. When two different galaxies collide, what type of galaxy is formed?

    A. An elliptical galaxy   B. An irregular galaxy

    C. A collision galaxy   D. A spiral galaxy

15. The word galaxy comes from the Greek word ----

    A. Galactic   B. Gale

    C. Gas   D. Milk

16. The Magellanic Clouds are

  A. Spiral galaxies
  B. Elliptical galaxies
  C. Large clouds of gas and dust
  D. Irregular galaxies

17. A galaxy of egg-shaped is called ---

  A. Irregular galaxy
  B. Oval shaped galaxy
  C. Elliptical galaxy
  D. Spiral galaxy

18. The andromeda galaxy is of what type?

  A. Elliptical
  B. Irregular
  C. Barred-spiral
  D. Spiral

19. At the center of our solar system is

  A. Dark matter
  B. A black hole
  C. A star
  D. The earth

20. What is the most distant object in the universe that is visible to the naked human eye?

  A. The Andromeda galaxy
  B. The Milky Way galaxy
  C. The Sun
  D. Moon

5. The Milky Way Galaxy

Quiz-4

1. The size of the milky way galaxy in terms of diameter?
   A. 5,000 light-years
   B. 10,000 light-years
   C. 100,000 light-years
   D. 1,000,000 light-years

2. Which galaxy is closest to the milky way galaxy?
   A. Andromeda galaxy
   B. Whirlpool
   C. Starburst
   D. Messier 8T

3. What best describes the shape of our galaxy?
   A. Spherical
   B. Spiral
   C. Elliptical
   D. Circular

4. Our galaxy contains how many stars and planets?
   A. 100 thousand
   B. 100 million
   C. 400 million
   D. 400 billion

5. The Milky Way has a halo of dark matter making up over
   A. 10% of its mass
   B. 55% of its mass
   C. 95% of its mass
   D. 99.99% of its mass

6. How many years does light take to cross from one side of the Milky Way to the other?
   A. 10,000 years
   B. 50,000 years
   C. 100,000 years
   D. 200,000 years

7. The Sun takes --- million years to orbit the Milky Way?
   A. 25 to 50
   B. 75 to 125
   C. 225 to 250
   D. 325 to 350

8. The shape of the Milky Way was discovered by ....

    A. Galileo Galilei   B. Edwin Hubble

    C. Aryabhata   D. Isaac Newton

9. The time taken by the Sun to orbit the Milky Way once is called a ---

    A. Lunar year   B. Light year

    C. Galactic Year   D. Calendar year

10. we can take a picture of the Milky Way from above

    A. True

    B. False

11. The largest galaxy in the Local group

    A. Andromeda   B. Triangulum

    C. Milky Way   D. Messier 8T

12. The second largest galaxy in the Local group?

    A. Andromeda   B. Milky Way

    C. Triangulum   D. Messier 8T

13. Which part of the milky way is the brightest?

    A. Centre Point   B. Galactic Centre

    C. Eye of the storm   D. Planetary Centre

14. How far is the Sun from the center of the Milky Way?

    A. 2 light years   B. 10 light years

    C. 2000 light years   D. 26000 light years

15. Within which spiral arm, the solar system is situated?

    A. Orion Arm   B. Perseus Arm

    C. Sagittarius Arm   D. White Arm

16. Which part of the Milky Way contains the oldest stars?

    A. Disk   B. Halo

    C. Galactic Centre   D. Nuclear Bulge

17. Where are globular clusters located in the Milky Way?

    A. Disk   B. Central bulge

    C. Halo   D. Spiral arms

18. What is the distance of the Sun from the centre of the Milky Way?

    A. 0.01 kiloparsec (kpc)   B. 1 kiloparsec

    C. 8 kiloparsec   D. 32 kiloparsec

19. How long does it take the Sun to complete one orbit of the Milky Way?

    A. 0.1 million years   B. 12 million years

    C. 230 million years   D. 1.2 billion years

20. Our Milky Way galaxy is a part of ---group

    A. Global   B. Local

    C. Galactic   D. Universal

6. Stars

Quiz-5

1. Massive self-luminous celestial bodies of superhot gas held together by their own gravity are called ---.

   A. Planets
   B. Comets
   C. Stars
   D. Moons

2. Only star in our solar system?

   A. Proxima Centauri
   B. The Sun
   C. Dog star
   D. Sirius

3. Which is the largest known star in the universe?

   A. The Sun
   B. Sirius
   C. Pole Star
   D. UY Scuti

4. Heavy stars go through --- before turning into black holes

   A. Supernova
   B. Big Bang
   C. Celestial event
   D. None of the above

5. Which star does not move in the sky?

   A. Altair
   B. Regulus
   C. Sirius
   D. Polaris

6. Massive self-luminous celestial bodies of superhot gas held together by their own gravity are called ---.

   A. Planets
   B. Comets
   C. Stars
   D. Moons

7. The nearest star to Earth (other than the sun) is ---

   A. Proxima Centauri
   B. Andromeda
   C. Betelgeuse
   D. Orion

8. The other name for Sirius, the brightest star in the sky?

A. Dog star   B. Pole star

C. North star   C. Carina

9. Which star is of the same class as our Sun?

A. Spica   B. Antares

C. Sirius   D. Tau Ceti

10. The process of star building which releases great amount of energy and radiation is known as

A. Fission   B. Fusion

C. Reaction   D. None of the above

11. How does the first stage of a star form?

A. A black hole   B. Asterism

C. A Stellar nebula   D. A Supernovae

12. Arrange the following colours of stars from coolest to hottest.

A. Blue, red, yellow, white

B. Red, yellow, white, blue

C. White, blue, red, yellow

D. Red, blue, yellow, white

13. What is a White Dwarf Star?

A. The collapsing star

B. A very small bright star.

C. A faint star of enormous density

D. A tiny star emitting energy

14. What is the fourth stage in the life cycle of an average star?

    A. Red giant   B. Pulsar

    C. Nebula.   D. Quasar

15. The biggest type of star is called?

    A. White dwarfs   B. Blue giants

    C. Red giants   D. Supergiants

16. Which color of the star is the hottest?

    A. Yellow   B. White

    C. Blue   D. Red

17. Which colour of the star is the coolest?

    A. Yellow   B. White

    C. Blue   D. Red

18. Stars are mostly made up of hydrogen and ---

    A. Oxygen   B. Helium

    C. Methane   D. Nitrogen

19. Stars spend 90 percent of their lives in their main sequence phase

    A. True

    B. False

20. At the end of the cycle of a star, it explodes in a catastrophic event. This is called ----

    A. Black holes   B. Dwarf

    C. Supernova   D. Extinction

Quiz-6

1. Identify the following star? Only star in our solar system

    A. Sirius   B. The Sun
    C. Pollux   D. Vega

2. The visible spots on the surface of the Sun are called?

    A. Hot spots   B. Bright spots
    C. White Patches   D. Sunspots

3. This star is the nearest star from Earth (Other than the Sun). can you name the star?

    A. Proxima centaury   B. Canopus
    C. Pollux   D. Vega

4. Identify the following star? It is also known as the Dog Star.

A. Deneb
B. Vega
C. Sirius-A
D. The Sun

5. Identify the following star? It is the second brightest star in the night sky from the Earth.

A. Sirius-A
B. Canopus
C. The Sun
D. Sirius-B

6. What do we call the star at 'A'? Here 'B' and 'C' are Little Dipper and Big Dipper respectively.

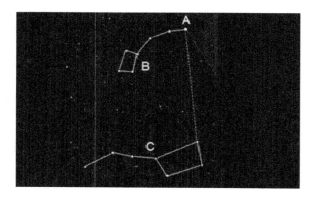

    A. North Star   B. Pole Star
    C. Deneb   D. Both 'A' and 'B'

A famous triangle formed by three stars is shown below. Answer the following questions.

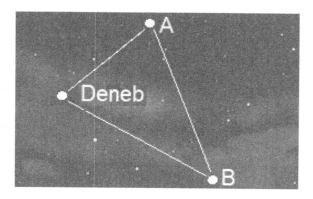

7. The triangle formed by joining the three stars 'A', 'B' and Deneb is called --

    A. Scalene triangle   B. Winter triangle
    C. Summer triangle   D. Night triangle

8. Name the star at 'A'
   A. Vega   B. Sirius-A
   C. Pollux   D. Altair

9. Which is the star at 'B'
   A. Sirius-B'   B. Sirius-B
   C. Altair   D. Vega

10. Which star in the summer triangle is biggest and most luminous?
    A. Altair   B. Pollux
    C. Vega   D. Deneb

11. What is the name this biggest star in the Universe?

   A. The Sun   B. UY Scuti
   C. VY Canis Majoris   D. Sirius-A

12. Which is the star 'P' in the constellation 'Gemini' as shown below

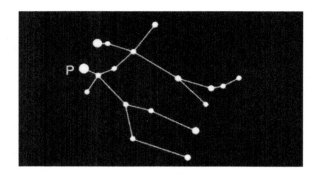

A. UY Scuti
B. VY Canis Majoris
C. Pollux
D. Deneb

Four stars are compared below including the star Sun. Answer following questions

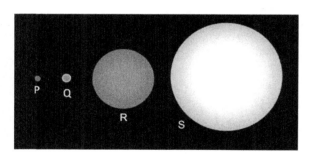

13. Identify the star at 'P'. It is probably the smallest possible star in the Milky way.

A. Proxima Centauri
B. 2mass J0523
C. Vega
D. The Sun

Four stars are compared below including the star Sun. Answer following questions

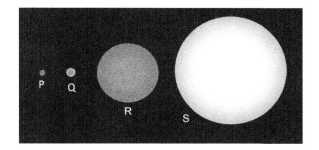

14. Name the star at 'Q'. It is the nearest star to the Earth. (other than the Sun)

   A. Proxima Centauri   B. Polaris
   C. Deneb   D. Sirius

15. Identify the star at 'R'. It is a G-type main-sequence star and closest to our planet Earth

   A. Vega   B. Pollux
   C. The Sun   D. Sirius-A

16. Identify the star at 'S'. It is about 1.8 times the size of the Sun. It is the brightest star in the night sky.

   A. Deneb   B. Sirius-A
   C. Proxima Centauri   D. Vega

Four hypergiants are compared below. These are VY Canis Majoris, Antares, UV Scuti and Betelgeuse. Identify these stars. Our star the Sun is also shown as a tiny dot.

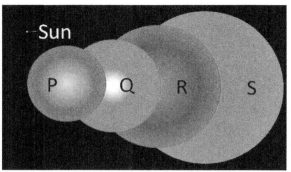

17. Identify the star UY Scuti? It's radius is about 1700 times than that of the Sun.

    A. P   B. R
    C. Q   D. S

18. Which star is VY Canis Majoris? It is a red hypergiant star?

    A. P   B. S
    C. R   D. Q

19. Which star is Antares? It is a red supergiant star

    A. P   B. Q
    C. R   D. S

20. Which star is Betelgeuse? It is a red supergiant star

    A. P   B. Q
    C. R   D. S

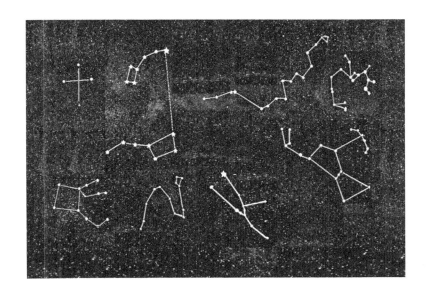

7. Constellations

Quiz-7

1. Zodiac constellations are constellations that lie
   - A. Along the plane of the ecliptic
   - B. On the southern hemisphere
   - C. Above the Milky Way
   - D. Inside the Milky way

2. Which of the following Southern zodiac constellation is located in the West?
   - A. Pisces
   - B. Aquarius
   - C. Aries
   - D. Taurus

3. The IAU officially listed how many modern and ancient constellations?
   - A. 44
   - B. 66
   - C. 88
   - D. 108

4. Which is the largest constellation?
   - A. Cetus
   - B. Hydra
   - C. Lyra
   - D. Libra

5. The largest of the Zodiac constellations is ---
   - A. Taurus
   - B. Pisces
   - C. Aries
   - D. Virgo

6. The second largest of the Zodiac constellations is ----
   - A. Pisces
   - B. Aquarius
   - C. Virgo
   - D. Taurus

7. The second largest of the 88 constellations is ----
   - A. Pisces
   - B. Aries
   - C. Virgo
   - D. Taurus

8. Aquarius represents

    A. The cupbearer to the   B. Nemean lion
       Greek Olympian gods

    C. Fish   D. Hunter

9. The smallest of the Zodiac constellations

    A. Leo   B. Scorpius

    C. Capricornus   D. Pisces

10. There are 13 official Zodiac constellations

    A. True

    B. False

11. The brightest star in the Zodiac constellations is?

    A. Spica   B. Aldebaran

    C. Pollux   D. Regulus

12. Which of the following constellation is called the 'Twins'

    A. Scorpius   B. Capricornus

    C. Gemini   D. Aquarius

13. The Aldebaran star is in which Zodiac Constellation?

    A. Virgo   B. Libra

    C. Taurus   D. Regulus

14. The constellations along the ecliptic are known as the constellations of the

    A. Perseus   B. Zodiac

    C. Cancer   D. Aries

15. The other name for constellation "The Crab" is?

    A. Pisces   B. Cancer

    C. Leo   D. Orion

16. What constellation is nicknamed "The Bull"?

   A. Taurus   B. Orion
   C. Leo   D. Ursa Major

17. Which constellation is referred to a mythological Greek hunter

   A. Orion   B. Leo
   C. Aries   D. Gemini

18. Which constellation is associated with the twins 'Castor and Pollux'.

   A. Orion   B. Leo
   C. Ursa Major   D. Gemini

19. Which constellation can be found between Aquarius and Aries

   A. Orion   B. Leo
   C. Pisces   D. Taurus

20. What constellation is nicknamed "The Ram"?

   A. Aries   B. Orion
   C. Leo   D. Pisces

Quiz-8

1. Which constellation is also known as "The Hare"?

   A. Lepus
   B. Leo
   C. Gemini
   D. Aries

2. Which constellation is nicknamed "The Twins"?

   A. Gemini
   B. Cancer
   C. Taurus
   D. Orion

3. Which of the following Zodiac constellations is called the Serpent Bearer

   A. Virgo
   B. Ophiuchus
   C. Aries
   D. Libra

4. There are 13 constellations in Zodiac. Astrologers use 12 of them. Which one is omitted?

   A. Ophiuchus
   B. Leo
   C. Aries
   D. Lepus

5. Which Zodiac constellations is associated with 'The goat'

   A. Virgo
   B. Ophiuchus
   C. Aries
   D. Capricornus

6. Which organization is responsible for naming constellations?

   A. The International Space Agency
   B. The International Astronomical Union
   C. NASA
   D. AIAA

7. Which Zodiac constellation is a representation of water?

   A. Libra
   B. Cancer
   C. Aquarius
   D. Virgo

8. Which constellation of the Zodiac has horns like a goat?

   A. Cancer
   B. Aries
   C. Capricornus
   D. Libra

9. The Zodiac constellation Cancer is nicknamed as?

   A. Lion
   B. Fish
   C. Scorpion
   D. Crab

10. The big dipper has how many stars?

    A. 7
    B. 8
    C. 9
    D. 10

11. Which Zodiac constellation is associated with Nemean lion?

    A. Libra
    B. Leo
    C. Gemini
    D. Cancer

12. Which is the only zodiac constellation in the sky represented by an inanimate object.

    A. Scorpius
    B. Gemini
    C. Cancer
    D. Libra

13. Which constellation contains one of the brightest stars Antares?

    A. Scorpius
    B. Libra
    C. Gemini
    D. Cancer

14. Which zodiac constellation is found between Aquarius and Aries?

    A. Leo
    B. Cancer
    C. Libra
    D. Pisces

15. Which Zodiac constellation's Latin name is Archer?

    A. Sagittarius   B. Leo
    C. Scorpius   D. Gemini

16. Which of these constellations is not in the zodiac?

    A. Aries   B. Virgo
    C. Lupus   D. Gemini

17. The brightest star in Orion?

    A. Saiph   B. Alnitak
    C. Rigel   D. Bellatrix

18. Which is the constellation only visible during the winter months?

    A. The Milky Way   B. Orion
    C. Gemini   D. Aries

19. Which of the following constellation is not in the zodiac?

    A. Alpha Centauri   B. Leo
    C. Aries   D. Capricornus

20. Sirius is found in which constellation?

    A. Andromeda   B. Canis Majoris
    C. Ursa Major   D. Ursa Minor

Quiz-9

1. Can you name the star at 'A'?

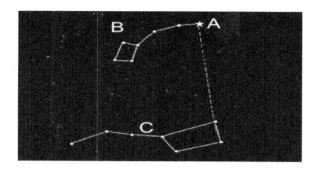

    A. Sirius-A   B. Pole star
    C. Proxima Centauri   D. Sirius-B

2. Identify the constellations at 'B' ?

    A. Canis Minor   B. Canis Major
    C. Ursa Major   D. Ursa Minor

3. Identify the constellation at 'C'?

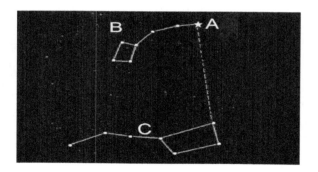

    A. Canis Major   B. Ursa Minor
    C. Big Dipper   D. Canis Minor

4. Name the following constellation?

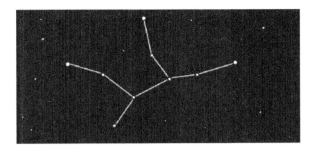

A. Libra B. Virgo
C. Leo   D. Gemini

5. Which is the following Zodiac constellation?

A. Cancer B. Virgo
C. Leo   D. Libra

6. Name the following constellation?

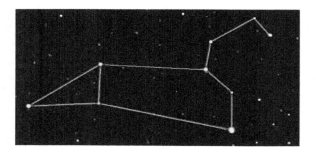

A. Gemini B. Virgo
C. Leo   D. Libra

7. Name the following Zodiac constellation?

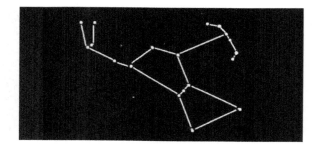

A. Orion   B. Big dipper
C. Canis Minor D. Virgo

44

8. Identify the following constellation?

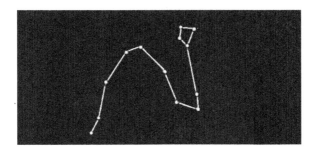

A. Aquarius   B. Libra
C. Pisces   D. Virgo

9. Which is the following Zodiac constellation?

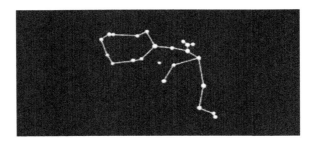

A. Aquarius   B. Gemini
C. Aries   D. Virgo

10. Which is the following constellation? It is the smallest Zodiac constellation?

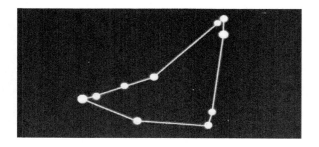

    A. Gemini   B. Virgo
    C. Capricornus   D. Taurus

11. Identify the following Zodiac constellation? Contains the brightest star 'Aldebaran'

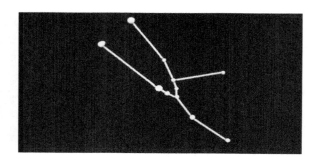

    A. Libra   B. Taurus
    C. Virgo   D. Gemini

12. Identify this constellation, the smallest of the 88 constellations?

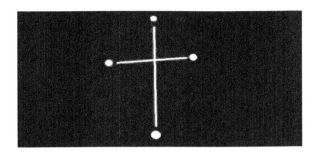

A. Aries
C. Leo
B. Crux
D. Orion

13. Identify this constellation, meaning 'Flying horse'?

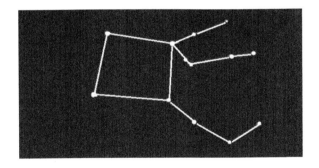

A. Pegasus
C. Gemini
B. Leo
D. Aries

14. Identify this constellation, which means 'Dragon'?

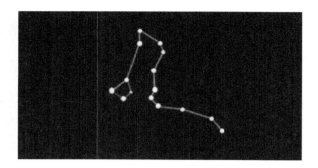

    A. Pegasus   B. Orion
    C. Draco   D. Leo

15. Identify this constellation, meaning 'Ram'?

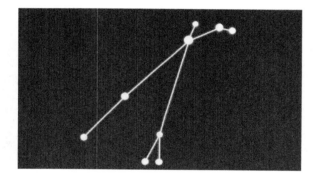

    A. Gemini   B. Orion
    C. Libra   D. Aries

16. Identify this constellation, lying between Virgo and Scorpius?

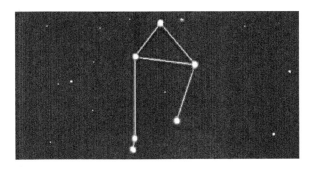

A. Crux   B. Leo
C. Libra   D. Gemini

17. Identify this constellation housing the brightest star in the night sky?

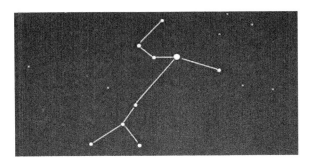

A. Canis Major   B. Ursa major
C. Virgo   D. Libra

49

18. Identify the star at 'A' in Canis major constellation (shown below)

A. Sirius
B. UY Scuti
C. Pollux
D. The Sun

19. Identify this constellation representing half man, half horse figure?

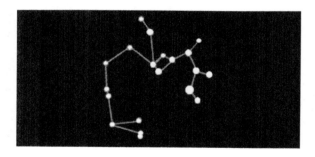

A. Orion
B. Aries
C. Libra
D. Sagittarius

50

20. Name this constellation? It is the biggest of 88 of constellation

A. Aries
B. Hydra
C. Gemini
D. Ursa Major

8. The Sun

Quiz-10

1. The only star in our solar system?

   A. Alpha Centauri   B. Sun

   C. Proxima Centauri   D. Sirius

2. What type of star is the sun today?

   A. White dwarf   B. Yellow dwarf

   C. Supergiant   D. Hypergiant

3. The thermonuclear reactions near the sun's center convert

   A. Hydrogen to Helium   B. Nitrogen to Helium

   C. Helium to Hydrogen   D. Helium to Nitrogen

4. How long has the sun existed in its present state?

   A. About 1 billion   B. About 2 billion

   C. About 4 billion   D. About 8 billion

5. Sun alone accounts for how much mass of the total mass in the Solar System?

   A. 25.8 %   B. 45.8 %

   C. 77.8 %   D. 99.8 %

6. What is the weight of the Sun as compared to Earth?

   A. 111,000 times   B. 222,000 times

   C. 333,000 times   D. 555,000 times

7. What is the diameter of the Sun compared to earth?

   A. 59 times   B. 89 times

   C. 109 times   D. 219 times

8. How many planet Earths can be fitted inside Sun?

   A. 0.3 million
   B. 1.3 million
   C. 3.3 million
   D. 6.3 million

9. What is the percentage of the mass of Earth compared to the mass of the Sun?

   A. 0.03 %
   B. 0.003%
   C. 0.0003%
   D. 0.00003%

10. The majority of the gas on Sun is ---

   A. Oxygen
   B. Hydrogen
   C. Nitrogen
   D. Helium

11. At what speed the Sun travels around the galactic center?

   A. 80 km/s
   B. 120 km/s
   C. 220 km/s
   D. 320 km/s

12. How many years does the Sun takes approximately to complete one orbit of the center of the Milky Way?

   A. 25-50 million years
   B. 100-125 million years
   C. 225-250 million years
   D. 350-450 million years

13. The Sun after completing its red giant phase will collapse. Then it will be known as a ---

   A. White Dwarf
   B. Orange Dwarf
   C. Dark Dwarf
   D. Black Dwarf

14. How much time does it take for the sunlight to reach Earth?

   A. 2 minutes 20 seconds
   B. 4 minutes 20 seconds
   C. 6 minutes 20 seconds
   D. 8 minutes 20 seconds

15. The atmosphere of the Sun is composed of three layers: the photosphere, the chromosphere, and the ---

   A. Troposphere   B. Corona

   C. Magma   D. Ionosphere

16. What is the temperature inside the Sun

   A. 5500°C   B. 15000° C

   C. 1 million° C   D. 15 million° C

17. Which of the following statements is correct?

   A. One day the Sun will consume the Earth
   B. The Sun rotates in the opposite direction to Earth
   C. The Sun rotates more quickly at its equator compared to its poles
   D. All of the above

18. What is a transient astronomical event called that causes the sudden appearance of a bright, apparently "new" star, that slowly fades over several weeks or many months?

   A. Nova   B. Nebula

   C. Volcano   D. Corona

19. What is the present age of the Sun?

   A. 4.6 thousand years   B. 4.6 million years

   C. 4.6 billion years   D. 4.6 trillion years

20. Viewing from Earth, why Sun and moon appears to be of the same size?

   A. Because of the disturbances due to atmosphere
   B. Both are of the same size
   C. The Sun is 400 times bigger than moon but also 400 times farther from Earth
   D. None of the above

Quiz-11

1. The outer atmosphere of the Sun marking the edge of the Sun's magnetic influence in space is called ----

   A. Magna-layer
   B. Ionosphere
   C. Magma
   D. Heliosphere

2. The solar wind streaming out in all directions from the rotating Sun is called

   A. Photosphere
   B. Magnetic plasma
   C. Heliosphere
   D. Solar-stream

3. The visible layer of the Sun about 100 km thick is called?

   A. Photosphere
   B. Magma
   C. Heliosphere
   D. Solar-stream

4. Which NASA's spacecraft has reached the innermost boundary of the Helios heath?

   A. Vostok-2
   B. Saturn-1
   C. Voyagers 1 and 2
   D. Discovery

5. The Sun consists of which of the following main gases

   A. 75% Hydrogen and 25% Helium
   B. 25% Hydrogen and 75% Helium
   C. 50% Hydrogen and 50% Helium
   D. None of the above

6. The minimum average distance between the Sun and Earth is ---

   A. 50 million km
   B. 100 million km
   C. 150 million km
   D. 400 million km

7. Nuclear fission that takes place in Sun converts

    A.   Hydrogen to Helium   B.   Helium to Hydrogen

    C.   Nitrogen to Hydrogen   D.   Oxygen to Hydrogen

8. Sun is also called

    A.   White dwarf   B.   Blue supergiant

    C.   Yellow star   D.   Red giant

9. The halo or crown of the Sun is the

    A.   Corona   B.   Ionosphere

    C.   Sunspots   D.   Heliosphere

10. The dark, planet-sized regions on the surface of the Sun caused by disturbances in the Sun's magnetic field are called ---

    A.   Darkspots   B.   Hotspots

    C.   Sunspots   D.   Photospots

11. Which statement is correct about the Sun?

    A.   It is made up of gases   B.   It has its own heat and light

    C.   Sun is a star   D.   All of the above

12. What is found at the center of the solar system?

    A.   Earth   B.   Mars

    C.   Sun   D.   Moon

13. The Sun is a star in which galaxy?

    A.   Pinwheel   B.   Andromeda

    C.   Sunflower   D.   The Milky Way

14. The Sunspots occur on which layer of the Sun?

    A.   Photosphere   B.   Ionosphere

    C.   Exosphere   D.   None of the above

15. The Sun makes up over --- of the mass in the Solar System.

    A.   1.8%   B.   23.5%

    C.   67.4%   D.   99.8%

16. The distance between the Sun and Earth is represented by

    A.   Solar Unit   B.   Light Year

    C.   Space Unit   D.   Astronomical Unit

17. The radius of our Sun is about --- the radius of biggest star UY Scuti

    A.   Same   B.   500 times

    C.   1/500 times   D.   1/1700 times

18. About how much longer will the Sun survive?

    A.   5 thousand years   B.   5 million years

    C.   5 billion years   D.   5 trillion years

19. The rotational period of the Sun on its axis is 27 days?

    A.   True   B.   False

20. The surface of the Sun is called photosphere

    A.   True   B.   False

9. Mercury

Quiz-12

1. The planet closest to Sun

   A. Venus   B. Mercury

   C. Mars   D. Earth

2. How many moons does Mercury have?

   A. 0   B. 1

   C. 2   D. 3

3. The smallest planet in our solar system ----

   A. Mercury   B. Venus

   C. Mars   D. Earth

4. How many days are there in a year on Mercury?

   A. 44   B. 66

   C. 88   D. 108

5. Mercury is ---- planet in the solar system

   A. Densest   B. Second densest

   C. Third densest   D. Least dense

6. The hottest planet in the solar system?

   A. Mercury   B. Venus

   C. Mars   D. Earth

7. The second hottest planet in the solar system

   A. Earth   B. Venus

   C. Mars   D. Mercury

8. The surface temperature on Mercury varies from

    A. 0 to 107°C   B. -50 to 227°C

    C. -107 to 317°C   D. -173 to 427°C

9. The most cratered planet in the Solar System.

    A. Mercury   B. Venus

    C. Mars   D. Neptune

10. There is no atmosphere on Mercury.

    A. True   B. False

11. Your weight on Earth is 100 kg; your weight on Mercury?

    A. 12 kg   B. 38 kg

    C. 54 kg   D. 88 kg

12. The orbital distance of Mercury is

    A. 0.26 AU   B. 0.39 AU

    C. 0.69 AU   D. 1 AU

13 A day on mercury is equal to earth days of 59

    A. True   B. False

14. Which planet has highest orbital eccentricity?

    A. Venus   B. Mercury

    C. Jupiter   D. Uranus

15. How many Earth days make one Mercury day?

    A. 125   B. 98.2

    C. 66.4   D. 58.6

16. In which two months do transits of Mercury occur?

    A. March and September   B. April and October

    C. May and November   D. June and December

17. The diameter of Mercury is --- the size of the Earth

    A. $3/4^{th}$ B. $2/5^{th}$

    C. Half   D. Similar to

18. NASA's spacecraft MESSENGER discovered --- on Mercury's north pole?

    A. Liquid methane   B. Water ice

    C. Helium   D. Liquid Nitrogen

19. Which moon in our solar system is bigger than Mercury?

    A. Callisto   B. Earth's moon

    C. Europa   D. Titan

20. The U.S. probe Mariner-10 visited Mercury in ---?

    A. 1958   B. 1968

    C. 1974   D. 1982

10. Venus

Quiz-13

1. Venus is ------ to Sun

   A. Nearest   B. Second closest

   C. Third closest   D. Fourth closest

2. How many moons does Venus have?

   A. 0   B. 1

   C. 2   D. 3

3. Which planet is almost the same size as of the Earth

   A. Mercury   B. Venus

   C. Mars   D. Uranus

4. One day on Venus is about ---- Earth days long

   A. 24   B. 146

   C. 243   D. 365

5. Which planet is considered as Earth's twin?

   A. Mercury   B. Venus

   C. Mars   D. Earth

6. The hottest planet in the solar system?

   A. Mercury   B. Venus

   C. Mars   D. Earth

7. The air on Venus mainly comprises of

   A. hydrogen   B. Oxygen

   C. Carbon dioxide   D. Helium

8. The surface temperature on Venus is about

    A. 107 deg C   B. 227 deg C

    C. 317deg C   D. 471deg C

9. Venus is ---- away from the Sun

    A. 0.5 AU   B. 0.7 AU

    C. 1.0 AU   D. 1.7 AU

10. A day on Venus lasts longer than a year on Venus

    A. True   B. False

11. If you weigh 100 kg on Earth, you will weigh on Venus as

    A. 12 kg   B. 38 kg

    C. 54 kg   D. 90 kg

12. The main composition of Venus atmosphere?

    A. Nitrogen and Helium   B. Carbon dioxide

    C. Hydrogen and helium   D. Oxygen and Hydrogen

13. Venus is the second-brightest natural object in the night sky after the Moon

    A. True   B. False

14. What is the surface pressure of air on Venus

    A. Same as that on earth   B. Twice of Earth

    C. 90 times of earth   D. Half of that on Earth

15. If 24 hours make one day on Earth, then how many hours will make one day on Venus?

    A. 528 hours   B. 1248 hours

    C. 3744 hours   D. 5832 hours

16. The symbol for Venus is ----

A. ♀   B. ♂̇

C. ♂   D. ♁

17. The diameter of Venus is about ----- than that of the Earth

A. 20.5%   B. 48.5%

C. 81.5%   D. 110.5%

18. How long is a Venus year?

A. 1 Earth day   B. 24 Earth days

C. 8 Earth days   D. 225 Earth days

19. Venus is named after the

A. Greek Queen   B. England queen

C. Roman goddess of love   D. Roman Queen

20. Sunlight reaches Venus in how many minutes?

A. 2 minutes   B. 4 minutes

C. 6 minutes   D. 8 minutes

11. The Earth

11.1 The Planet Earth
Quiz-14

1. Earth is the ---- planet from the Sun

   A. Second   B. Third

   C. Fourth   D. Fifth

2. The Earth is the smallest of the terrestrial planets?

   A. True   B. False

3. Earth is the only planet not named on any deity?

   A. True   B. False

4. What is the age of Earth?

   A. 33 thousand years   B. 4.62 million years

   C. 4.54 billion years   D. 56.68 billion years

5. The difference between the equatorial and polar diameter of Earth is ---

   A. 14 km   B. 43 km

   C. 103 km   D. 416 km

6. The magnetic field protects the Earth from the effects of solar winds

   A. True   B. False

7. Which is the densest planet of the solar system?

   A. Earth   B. Jupiter

   C. Saturn   D. Mars

8. What percentage of Earth is covered with water?

   A. 40% B. 50%

   C. 60% D. 70%

9. Earth takes about 23 hours, 56 minutes and 4 seconds to rotate about its axis

   A. True B. False

10. The Earth is between the planets Venus and Mars

   A. True B. False

11. How far is the Earth from the Sun in Angstrom Unit (AU)?

   A. 0.1 AU B. 0.5 AU

   C. 1.0 AU D. 150 AU

12. What's the percentage of oxygen on Earth?

   A. 7% B. 21%

   C. 44% D. 79%

13. The seasonal variations on Earth are due to the ---

   A. Stratosphere B. Greenhouse effect

   C. Tilt of Earth's axis D. Presence of Moon

14. The average orbital speed of Earth?

   A. 0.298 km/s B. 2.98 km/s

   C. 29.8 km/s D. 298 km/s

15. What is the circumference of the Earth at equator?

   A. 10,075 km B. 20,075 km

   C. 30,075 km D. 40,075 km

16. What is the speed of Earth rotation on the equator?

    A.   265 m/s   B.   365 m/s

    C.   465 m/s   D.   565 m/s

17. The number of moons of Earth?

    A.   0   B.   1

    C.   2   D.   3

18. The movement of the earth on its axis is called?

    A.   Revolution   B.   Rotation

    C.   Movement   D.   Cycle

19. The movement of the earth around the sun's orbit is called ----

    A.   Torque   B.   Rotation

    C.   Revolution   D.   Movement

20. The earth takes about ---- to complete one revolution around the Sun

    A.   23.98 hours   B.   48.5 hours

    C.   1 month   D.   365.25 days

Quiz-15

1. A leap year on Earth repeats after ----

   A. 1 year
   B. 2 year
   C. 3 year
   D. 4 year

2. What is the distance of the geostationary orbit of the earth from the earth's surface?

   A. 36 km
   B. 360 km
   C. 3600 km
   D. 36000 km

3. All the planets revolve around the Sun in an ---- path

   A. circular
   B. elliptical
   C. square
   D. Straight

4. The only planet known to harbor life is ----

   A. Earth
   B. Venus
   C. Saturn
   D. Mars

5. What is the correct composition of air?

   A. Oxygen 78%, nitrogen 21%, other gases 1%
   B. Nitrogen 78%, oxygen 21%, other gases 1%
   C. Carbon 78%, oxygen 21%, nitrogen 1%.
   D. Nitrogen 70%, oxygen 29%, other gases 1%

6. The gravitational interaction between Earth and the Moon causes ---

   A. Seasons
   B. tides
   C. Atmosphere
   D. Volcanos

7. The fifth-largest planet in the solar system?

A. Earth   B. Venus

C. Saturn   D. Uranus

8. What is the average radius of Earth?

A. 3240 Km   B. 4600 Km

C. 5400 Km   D. 6400 Km

9. The diameter of earth is about ---- smaller than the Sun

A. 49 times   B. 78 times

C. 109 times   D. 1,330 times

10. What is the symbol of the Earth?

A. ♀   B. ♂

C. ☿   D. ♀

11. The average distance of the earth from the Sun is ----

A. 100 million km   B. 150 million km

C. 220 million km   D. 450 million km

12. The mass of Earth is

A. 5.97×10^{14} kg   B. 5.97×10^{18} kg

C. 5.97×10^{24} kg   D. 5.97×10^{34} kg

13. The largest terrestrial planet in the solar system?

A. Earth   B. Venus

C. Saturn   D. Uranus

14. Which statement is/are correct about Earth?

A. Earth has a powerful magnetic field.

B. It has only one natural satellite

C. Earth is the only planet not named after a god.

D. All of the above

15. The speed of rotation of Earth is highest at?

A. Arctic Circle   B. North Pole

C. Equator   D. South Pole

16. What is the equatorial circumference of the earth?

A. 30,000 Km   B. 35,000 Km

C. 40,000 Km   D. 45,000 Km

17. The shape of Earth is ---

A. Spherical   B. Flat

C. Oblate spheroid   D. Elliptical

18. The Earth rotates around its axis from …

A. North to South   B. South to North

C. East to West   D. West to East

19. The Earth and --- are often called planetary twins

A. Venus   B. Mercury

C. Mars   D. Neptune

20. This layer on Earth's atmosphere protects us from the ultraviolet rays of the Sun?

A. Ozone layer   B. Oxygen layer

C. Nitrogen layer   D. Hydrogen layer

11.2 The Interior of the Earth
Quiz-16

1. The innermost layer inside the Earth is called the ----
   - A. Inner core
   - B. Inner crust
   - C. Inner mantle
   - D. Initial core

2. The layer which extends up to 2,900 km below Earth's outer crust ...
   - A. Crust
   - B. Core
   - C. Mantle
   - D. Exosphere

3. How hot is the Earth's inner core?
   - A. 540°C
   - B. 1100°C
   - C. 6000°C
   - D. 5 million°C

4. The Earth's inner core is made up of what two metals?
   - A. Iron and Zinc
   - B. Iron and Nickel
   - C. Aluminum and Copper
   - D. Copper and Bronze

5. The hot molten rock found inside the Earth is called ----
   - A. Ionosphere
   - B. core
   - C. Magma
   - D. Lava

6. Which method do we generally use for determining the structure of the earth's interior?
   - A. Core samples
   - B. Magma sample
   - C. Magnetic field
   - D. Seismology

7. Earth's outer layer is called ----
   - A. Lithosphere
   - B. Troposphere
   - C. Ionosphere
   - D. Exosphere

8. From interior to surface, the correct sequence of Earth

A. Core >Crust >Mantle
B. Mantle >Core >Curst
C. Crust >Mantle >Core
D. Core >Mantle >Crust

9. What do you call the molten rock before it gets erupted?

A. Magma
B. Lava
C. Crust
D. Rock

10. The molten rock erupting out of volcano is called ---

A. Lava
B. Gas
C. Mantle
D. Crust

11. The outer layer of Earth is called ----

A. Core
B. Mantle
C. Crust
D. Troposphere

12. As you go deeper inside the Earth ----

A. It gets cooler, the material gets denser, and pressure increases
B. It gets hotter, the material gets denser, and pressure decreases
C. It gets hotter, the material gets denser, and pressure increases
D. It gets cooler, the material gets denser, and pressure decreases

13. Which layer is mostly made up of Oxygen and Silicon?

A. Lithosphere
B. Crust
C. Mantle
D. Troposphere

14. The inner core spins at a different speed to the rest of the planet causing the ---

A. Earth's magnetic field
B. Seasons on Earth
C. Earth's Rotation
D. None of these

15. The magnetic field helps to protect the Earth from

A. Greenhouse effect   B. Sun's solar winds

C. Lightening   D. Plasma

16. The innermost part of the core is primarily a solid ball of radius ----

A. 610 km   B. 1220 km

C. 2410 km   D. 3220 km

17. The layer of the Earth on which we walk every day is called

A. Crust   B. Mantle

C. Outer Core   D. Inner Core

18. The thickness of the crust is about ...

A. 2 km thick under the oceans and about 12 km thick under the continents

B. 8 km thick under the oceans and about 35 km thick under the continents

C. 32 km thick under the oceans and about 12 km thick under the continents

D. 12 km thick under the oceans as well as under the continents

19. The radius of Earth's inner core is about --- of Earth's radius

A. 5%   B. 10%

C. 20%   D. 45%

20. The crust and the upper layer of the mantle together is called the ---

A. Lithosphere   B. Troposphere

C. Exosphere   D. Ionosphere

11.3 Geographical Features of Earth
Quiz-17

1. What percentage of all the water on Earth is considered freshwater?

   A. 3%
   B. 10.8%
   C. 21%
   D. 47%

2. How much of Earth's surface is land, consisting of continents and islands?

   A. 29%
   B. 11%
   C. 38%
   D. 71%

3. The largest ocean on earth?

   A. The Atlantic Ocean
   B. The Pacific Ocean
   C. The Indian Ocean
   D. The Arctic Ocean

4. What is the name of the deepest location in the world's oceans?

   A. Mariana Trench
   B. Deep point
   C. Barrier Reef
   D. Dark spot

5. Name the highest mountain on earth?

   A. Mount Makalu
   B. Mount K2
   C. Mount Everest
   D. Mount Manaslu

6. The longest river on Earth?

   A. Amazon
   B. Mississippi
   C. Nile
   D. Ganges

7. The largest continent on Earth?

    A. Africa

    B. Asia

    C. Europe

    D. America

8. Largest island on Earth?

    A. Island

    B. Switzerland

    C. England

    D. Greenland

9. Smallest continent on Earth?

    A. Australia

    B. Africa

    C. Asia

    D. America

10. The world's largest desert is ---?

    A. Sahara

    B. Thar

    C. Gobi

    D. Kalahari

11. Deepest Ocean on Earth?

    A. Arctic Ocean

    B. Indian Ocean

    C. Atlantic Ocean

    D. Pacific Ocean

12. The deepest lake on Earth?

    A. Caspian Sea

    B. Lake Malawi

    C. Lake Dal

    D. Lake Baikal

13. The largest river in the world?

    A. Amazon

    B. Mississippi

    C. Nile

    D. Ganges

14. Your weight on the equator will be more than that at poles

    A. True

    B. False

15. What was the lowest temperature ever recorded on Earth at Vostok Station in 1983?

    A. - 48° C
    B. -69.2° C
    C. -89.2° C
    D. -100°C

16. What was the hottest temperature ever recorded on Earth at Libya in 1922?

    A. 37.8°C
    B. 47.8°C
    C. 57.8°C
    D. 67.8°C

17. The lowest point in the world?

    A. Dead sea
    B. Caspian Sea
    C. Deep-sea
    D. Blue sea

18. Which of the following is not a continent?

    A. Antarctica
    B. Greenland
    C. Australia
    D. America

19. Classify the following oceans from smallest to largest

    A. The Arctic Ocean, The Indian Ocean, The Atlantic Ocean, The Pacific Ocean
    B. The Arctic Ocean, The Atlantic Ocean, The Indian Ocean, The Pacific Ocean
    C. The Pacific Ocean, The Arctic Ocean, The Indian Ocean, The Atlantic Ocean
    D   The Arctic Ocean, The Pacific Ocean, The Atlantic Ocean, The Indian Ocean

20. Classify the following continents from largest to smallest

    A. America, Asia, Australia, Africa
    B. Africa, America, Asia, Australia
    C. Asia, America, Africa, Australia
    D. Asia, Africa, America, Australia

11.4 Seasons on Earth

Quiz-18

1. Earth's axis of rotation is tilted with respect to its orbital plane, producing ----
   - A. Eco balance
   - B. Tides
   - C. Atmosphere
   - D. Seasons on Earth

2. What is the angle of inclination of Earth's Axis with the perpendicular line to the orbital plane?
   - A. 12.2 deg
   - B. 23.5 deg
   - C. 45.0 deg
   - D. 75.4 deg

3. The angle of inclination of Earth's Axis with its orbital plane is?
   - A. 26½ degree
   - B. 46¾ Degree
   - C. 66½ degree
   - D. 90 degree

4. In June solstice, the ---- is tilted toward the Sun
   - A. North Pole
   - B. South Pole
   - C. The tropic of Cancer
   - D. The equator

5. Summer Solstice is ----
   - A. July 23rd
   - B. March 21st
   - C. October 22nd
   - D. June 21st

6. In June solstice, the ---- Hemisphere gets more of the Sun's direct rays
   - A. Southern
   - B. Northern
   - C. Eastern
   - D. Western

7. Leap year consists of ---- days
   A. 364   B. 365
   C. 366   D. 367

8. The Northern Hemisphere is tilted towards the Sun on ---
   A. 21st March   B. 22nd May
   C. 21st June   D. 22nd Dec

9. What is meant by Equinox?
   A. South Pole is tilted towards Sun
   B. Neither of the poles is tilted towards the sun
   C. North Pole is tilted towards Sun
   D. North Poles are tilted towards Equator

10. North pole is pointed towards the Sun when the Northern hemisphere is experiencing winter?
    A. True   B. False

11. The longest day and the shortest night occur on ----
    A. 21st February   B. 22nd May
    C. 21st June   D. 22nd October

12. What is the meaning of the term 'Equinox'?
    A. Equal day   B. Equal night
    C. Equal solar eclipse   D. Equal lunar eclipse

13. The day in the Northern Hemisphere on which the North Pole leans to the Sun is called ---
    A. Summer Solstice   B. Winter Equinox
    C. Fall Equinox   D. Spring Solstice

14. The day on which the Northern and Southern hemispheres receive an equal amount of sunlight is called ---

A. Summer Solstice   B. Spring Equinox

C. Winter Solstice   D. Autumnal Equinox

15. During which season do the leaves change color and fall off the trees?

A. Spring   B. Summer

C. Autumn   D. Winter

16. In June solstice, the ---- Hemisphere points away from the Sun

A. Southern   B. Northern

C. Eastern   D. Western

17. During which season do most plants begin to grow and many animals have their babies?

A. Spring   B. Summer

C. Autumn   D. Winter

18. At poles, sun does not rise or set for about

A. A year   B. Half a year

C. One month   D. Two years

19. The northern hemisphere tilts towards the sun during

A. Summer   B. Winter

C. Autumn   D. Spring

20. The Earth revolves ----- around the Sun?

A. Clockwise   B. Anti-clockwise

C. Linearly   D. Tangentially

Quiz-19

1. In one year (365 1/4 days), the Earth makes one complete

   A. Rotation
   B. Revolution
   C. Angular motion
   D. Oscillation

2. In one day (24 hours), the Earth makes one complete

   A. Rotation
   B. Revolution
   C. Angular motion
   D. Oscillation

3. In the Northern hemisphere, the sun is directly above ---- during summer solstice?

   A. Tropic of Capricorn
   B. Equator
   C. Tropic of cancer
   D. South pole

4. Which of the following best describes equinoxes?

   A. The southern hemisphere is tilted toward the Sun
   B. The earth is tilted neither toward nor away from the Sun
   C. The northern hemisphere is tilted away from the Sun
   D. The northern hemisphere is tilted toward the Sun

5. The sun does not set above the arctic circle on the day of the summer solstice.

   A. True
   B. False

6. In June Solstice during summer, we feel hot because the Sun is nearest to the Earth

   A. True
   B. False

7. What percentage of insolation is received by the earth's surface?

   A. 23%
   B. 36%
   C. 51%
   D. 88%

8. What is the position of the Earth in its orbit, when it is at its greatest distance from the Sun causing summer in the Northern Hemisphere?

   A. Perihelion
   B. Aphelion
   C. Apogee
   D. Perigee

9. What is the maximum length of a day on the poles?

   A. 12 hours
   B. 1 day
   C. 3 months
   D. 6 months

10. Equinox occurs when the Sun is vertically above

   A. Tropic of Capricorn
   B. Tropic of Cancer
   C. Poles
   D. Equator

11. Days and nights are equal throughout the globe when Sun is above

   A. Poles
   B. Tropic of Cancer
   C. Equator
   D. Tropic of Capricorn

12. Heat received by earth from the Sun is known as

   A. Insolation
   B. Solar convection
   C. Solar radiation
   D. Thermal currents

13. The speed of rotation of the earth is highest at the ---

   A. Arctic circle
   B. Equator
   C. North pole
   D. Tropic of Cancer

14. The speed of revolution of Earth is ----

   A. 10 km/s
   B. 20 km/s
   C. 30 km/s
   D. 40.5 km/s

15. Green House Effect means ----

   A. Urban pollution
   B. Deforestation.
   C. Trapping of solar energy due to atmospheric carbon dioxide
   D. Trapping. of solar energy due to atmospheric oxygen

Answer questions from 16 to 19 by referring following figure

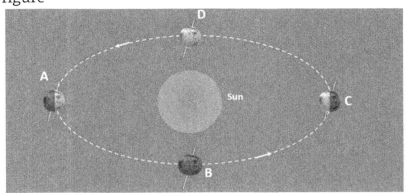

16. Summer Solstice is represented by ---

    A. A B. B
    C. C D. D

17. The September Equinox is represented by----

    A. A B. B
    C. C D. D

18. 'C' represents

    A. Summer Solstice B. December Solstice
    C. September Equinox D. March Equinox

19. 'D' represents

    A. Summer Solstice B. December Solstice
    C. September Equinox D. March Equinox

20. The tropic of Cancer does not pass-through India

    A. True B. False

11.5 The Earth's Atmosphere

Quiz-20

1. We live in --- layer of the atmosphere?

   A. Troposphere   B. Stratosphere

   C. Mesosphere   D. Exosphere

2. The coldest region of Earth's atmosphere is ---

   A. Mesosphere   B. Exosphere

   C. Stratosphere   D. Troposphere

3. What is the percentage of Nitrogen in the earth's atmosphere?

   A. 0.03 %   B. 21.29%

   C. 78.08%   D. 92.36%

4. Which types of the cloud mean the Latin word for rain?

   A. Stratus   B. Nimbus

   C. Cumulus   D. Cirrus

5. Which is the most abundant element in the earth's atmosphere?

   A. Argon   B. Carbon-di-oxide

   C. Nitrogen   D. Oxygen

6. What is the percentage of Oxygen in earth's atmosphere?

   A. 0.03 %   B. 20.95 %

   C. 78.09%   D. 92.36%

7. Argon is the third major constitutes of air by volume. Its percentage in air is about

   A. 41%   B. 21%

   C. 5.07%   D. 0.93%

8. Passenger jet aircrafts fly normally at what altitude?

   A. 5 km
   B. 11 km
   C. 18 km
   D. 30 km

9. The amount of actual water vapour of air is known as ---

   A. Absolute humidity
   B. Relative humidity
   C. Dew point
   D. None of these

10. Aeroplanes fly normally in the stratosphere layer

    A. Stratosphere
    B. Troposphere
    C. Ionosphere
    D. Aerosphere

11. What is the correct order of sequence of layers of the atmosphere from earth's surface upwards

    A. Troposphere, Stratosphere, Ionosphere, Mesosphere
    B. Troposphere, Stratosphere, Mesosphere, Ionosphere
    C. Stratosphere, Troposphere, Ionosphere, Mesosphere
    D. Stratosphere, Troposphere, Mesosphere, Ionosphere

12. In which layer of the atmosphere, the temperature increases dramatically?

    A. Ionosphere
    B. Exosphere
    C. Stratosphere
    D. Troposphere

13. The height of the troposphere layer of the atmosphere is from Earth up to ---

    A. 8 km
    B. 12 km
    C. 18 km
    D. 30 km

14. The border line separating Earth's atmosphere to space is called ---

    A. Space line
    B. Limit line
    C. Karman line
    D. Barrier line

15. Which layer of the atmosphere contains the highest density of gas molecules?

    A. Mesosphere   B. Stratosphere

    C. Thermosphere   D. Troposphere

16. With an increase in altitude, the atmospheric pressure ---

    A. Decreases   B. Increases

    C. Remains constant   D. First decreases then increases

17. Which layer of the atmosphere contains the ozone layer?

    A. Exosphere   B. Mesosphere

    C. Stratosphere   D. Thermosphere

18. In which layer the all-weather phenomena take place?

    A. Mesosphere   B. Stratosphere

    C. Thermosphere   D. Troposphere

19. In which layer of the Earth's atmosphere, most meteors burn up upon entry?

    A. Exosphere   B. Thermosphere

    C. Mesosphere   D. Stratosphere

20. Which is the outermost layer of the Earth's atmosphere?

    A. Exosphere   B. Thermosphere

    C. Mesosphere   D. Stratosphere

12. Mars

Quiz-21

1. Mars is the ---- planet from the Sun

   A. Second   B. Third

   C. Fourth   D. Fifth

2. Mars is often referred as the ---- Planet?

   A. Brown   B. Red

   C. Pink   D. Orange

3. What is the orbital period of Mars?

   A. 156 days   B. 365 days

   C. 452 days   D. 687 days

4. Mars is the second-smallest planet in the Solar System

   A. True   B. False

5. The diameter of Mars is about ---- than that of the Earth

   A. 0.246 times   B. 0.532 times

   C. 0.886 times   D. 1.23 times

6. Compared to Earth, the volume of Mars is

   A. 0.0614 times of Earth   B. 0.151 times of Earth

   C. 0.336 times of Earth   D. 0.55 times of Earth

7. Compared to Earth, the mass of Mars is

   A. 0.107 times of Earth   B. 0.264 times of Earth

   C. 0.336 times of Earth   D. 0.500 times of Earth

8. Mars carries the name of the ----

    A. Roman god of war   B. Roman god of peace

    C. Roman god of harvest   D. Roman god of fire

9. The reddish appearance of Mars is due to ---

    A. Reddish fire on Mars   B. Iron Oxide

    C. Zinc Sulphate   D. Sulphur di-oxide

10. Mars is smaller than Mercury

    A. True   B. False

11. Mars is a/an ----

    A. Ice Giant   B. Gas giant

    C. Muddy planet   D. Terrestrial planet

12. Mars has how many moons?

    A. 0   B. 1

    C. 2   D. 3

13. Which of the followings is a moon of Mars?

    A. Phobos   B. Triton

    C. Io   D. None

14. Average orbital speed of Mars?

    A. 6 km/s   B. 11 km/s

    C. 24 km/s   D. 44 km/s

15. The first spacecraft to visit Mars?

    A. Vostok-1   B. Mariner-4

    C. Apollo-7   D. Soyuz-2

16. What is the symbol of Mars?

A. ♀

B. ♂

C. ♆

D. ☿

17. The atmosphere of Mars consists of about 96% of ----

A. Carbon di-oxide

B. Argon

C. Nitrogen

D. Oxygen

18. The axis tilt of Mars is similar to that of the Earth's

A. True

B. False

19. Mars's average distance from the Sun is roughly ----

A. 0.5 AU

B. 1.0 AU

C. 1.5 AU

D. 2.0 AU

20. If your weight on Earth is 100 kg. Your weight on Mars will be ----

A. 12 kg

B. 38 kg

C. 49 kg

D. 62 kg

13. Jupiter

Quiz-22

1. Jupiter is the ---- planet from the Sun

   A. Third
   B. Fourth
   C. Fifth
   D. Sixth

2. Jupiter is the largest planet in our solar system?

   A. True
   B. False

3. Jupiter's radius is about ---- times the radius of the Sun

   A. 1/2
   B. 1/10
   C. 1/50
   D. 1/100

4. Mass of Jupiter is ----

   A. 1/1047 times of Sun
   B. 2.5 times of all other planets in the Solar System combined
   C. 318 times of Earth
   D. All of the above

5. The best-known feature of Jupiter is the

   A. Great Red Spot
   B. Dusty atmosphere
   C. Giant Rocks
   D. Volcanos

6. The four largest moons of Jupiter are known as ----

   A. Jupiter moons
   B. Giant moons
   C. Galilean moons
   D. Outer moons

7. The largest moon of Jupiter is Europa?

   A. Europa
   B. Ganymede
   C. Callisto
   D. Io

8. The number of moons of Jupiter?

   A. 44   B. 58

   C. 79   D. 92

9. The diameter of Jupiter is ---bigger than that of the Earth

   A. 3.7 times   B. 8.2 times

   C. 11.2 times   D. 15.9 times

10. A "day" on Jupiter is 9.8 hours long

    A. True   B. False

11. If your weight on Earth is 100 kg. What will be your weight on Jupiter?

    A. 253 kg   B. 195 kg

    C. 100 kg   D. 58 kg

12. Which are the closest neighboring planets of Jupiter?

    A. Saturn and Uranus   B. Uranus and Neptune

    C. Earth and Saturn   D. Mars and Saturn

13. Which famous comet crashed into Jupiter in 1994?

    A. Halley's comet   B. Hale-Bopp

    C. Shoemaker-Levy 9   D. Comet Encke

14. How many Earths can be fitted inside Jupiter?

    A. 462   B. 607

    C. 984   D. 1300

15 Which asteroid group shares a path with Jupiter around the Sun?

    A. Flora   B. Trojans

    C. Jovian   D. Nysa

16. Jupiter orbits the Sun at a distance of -----

    A. 0.78 AU   B. 1.0 AU

    C. 5.2 AU   D. 7.8 AU

17. Jupiter has how many rings?

    A. 0   B. 2

    C. 4   D. 6

18. Who discovered Jupiter's Great Red Spot?

    A. Galileo Galilei   B. Giovanni Cassini

    C. Copernicus   D. Johannes Kepler

19. Who discovered the four largest moons of Jupiter?

    A. Copernicus   B. Galileo Galilei

    C. Isaac Newton   D. Johannes Kepler

20. What is the name of a permanent hurricane on Jupiter that is as wide as three Earths?

    A. The volcanic Spot   B. The Great Gas Spot

    C. The Great Red spot   D. The giant hurricane spot

14. Saturn

Quiz-23

1. Saturn is the ---- planet from the Sun

   A. 2nd   B. 4th

   C. 6th   D. 8th

2. Saturn is the third largest planet in our solar system.

   A. True   B. False

3. How many Earths side by side would almost span Saturn's diameter (excluding Saturn's rings)

   A. 4   B. 7

   C. 9   D. 11

4. Saturn is a massive ball made mostly of …

   A. Hydrogen and Oxygen   B. Helium and Nitrogen

   C. Argon and Helium   D. Hydrogen and Helium

5. Saturn orbits at a distance of about---- from the Sun

   A. 9.5 AU   B. 11.5 AU

   C. 13.5 AU   D. 15.5 AU

6. Saturn is a ---- planet and therefore does not have a solid surface like Earth's

   A. Gas-giant   B. Rocky

   C. Icy   D. Terrestrial

7. Saturn has the most spectacular ----

   A. Rocky system   B. Ring system

   C. Volcano system   D. Stormy system

8. How many moons does Saturn have?

   A. 26   B. 54

   C. 82   D. 108

9. Which spacecraft orbited Saturn 294 times from 2004 to 2017

   A. Pioneer   B. Apollo

   C. Vostok   D. Cassini

10. The Cassini spacecraft was intentionally vaporized on Saturn's atmosphere in 2017.

    A. True   B. False

11. The rings we see on Saturn are made of chunks of ----

    A. Ice and rock   B. Solar storm

    C. Volcanic storm   D. Nitrogen gases

12. Saturn takes about ---- to rotate on its axis once

    A. 6.8 hours   B. 10.7 hours

    C. 22.8 hours   D. 76.8 hours

13. Saturn takes --- Earth years to orbit the sun.

    A. 6   B. 29

    C. 58   D. 86

14. The only planet, whose average density is less than water

    A. Jupiter   B. Mars

    C. Saturn   D. Neptune

15. Saturn diameter is ---- times bigger than that of Earth

    A. 2.2

    B. 4.8

    C. 9.5

    D. 12.2

16. The mass of Saturn is equal to --- than that of the Earth

    A. 33 times

    B. 52 times

    C. 71 times

    D. 95 times

17. The thickness of Saturn rings is about 30 to 300 feet

    A. True

    B. False

18. How many rings does Saturn have?

    A. 3

    B. 5

    C. 7

    D. 21

19. The largest moon of Saturn is ----

    A. Titan

    B. Ganymede

    C. Anthe

    D. Calypso

20. Earth is --- times as dense as Saturn

    A. 0.25

    B. 0.5

    C. 4

    D. 8

15. Uranus

Quiz-24

1. Uranus is the ---- planet in the Solar System

   A. Smallest   B. largest

   C. Second largest   D. Third Largest

2. Uranus is the ---- planet from the Sun

   A. 3rd   B. 5th

   C. 7th   D. 8th

3. The diameter of Uranus is ----- times than that of Earth

   A. 0.75   B. 1.75

   C. 3.75   D. 6.75

4. How many hours make one day on Uranus?

   A. 17   B. 28

   C. 36   D. 48

5. The mass of Uranus is 14.5 times higher than Earth

   A. 14.5   B. 18.6

   C. 20.4   D. 22.5

6. Uranus takes 84 years to complete one orbit of the Sun.

   A. True   B. False

7. The planet Uranus was discovered by ---

   A. William Herschel   B. Nicolaus Copernicus

   C. Galileo Galilei   D. Johannes Kepler

8. What chemical gives Uranus its blue-green color?

   A. Hydrogen   B. Nitrogen

   C. Methane   D. Helium

9. Uranus is a mainly composed of ----

   A. Hydrogen and Helium   B. Nitrogen and Helium

   C. Helium and Argon   D. Hydrogen and Oxygen

10. Uranus' axis of rotation is lying on its side .

   A. True   B. False

11. Uranus axis tilt is ----

   A. 3.4 degrees   B. 23.4 degrees

   C. 98 degrees   D. 118 degrees

12. Uranus has 13 rings.

   A. True   B. False

13. What is the average distance of Uranus from the Sun?

   A. 11 AU   B. 19 AU

   C. 27 AU   D. 46 AU

14. Many moons of Uranus are named after ----

   A. Roman Gods   B. Greek Gods

   C. Characters in William   D. Egyptian Gods
      Shakespeare plays and
      Alexander Pope poems

15 Which is the brightest moon of Uranus?

    A. Oberon   B. Titania

    C. Miranda   D. Ariel

16. How many moons does Uranus have?

    A. 17   B. 27

    C. 37   D. 47

17. The largest moon of Uranus?

    A. Oberon   B. Miranda

    C. Titania   D. Ariel

18. When English astronomer William Herschel first saw
Uranus, he thought it was ----

    A. A Star   B. A Comet

    C. An Asteroid   D. Meteor

19. Uranus has the largest tilt in our Solar System

    A. True   B. False

20. The first planet discovered through a telescope?

    A. Mars   B. Jupiter

    C. Saturn   D. Uranus

16. Neptune

Quiz-25

1. Neptune is the ---- planet from the Sun

   A. First   B. Third

   C. Sixth   D. Last

2. The diameter of Neptune is ---- bigger than the Earth

   A. 0.5 times   B. 1.6 times

   C. 3.7 times   D. 8.4 times

3. The planet Neptune was discovered on ----

   A. 23 September 1746   B. 23 September 1846

   C. 23 September 1946   D. None of the above

4. A day on Neptune is --- hours long.

   A. 16   B. 24

   C. 32   D. 64

5. Neptune takes ---- to complete one orbit of the Sun

   A. 42 years   B. 117 years

   C. 165 years   D. 365 years

6. Neptune is a ---- composed of hydrogen and helium

   A. Terrestrial planet   B. Gas giant

   C. Rocky planet   D. Icy planet

7. Neptune's largest moon?

   A. Triton   B. Titan

   C. Atlas   D. Ganymede

8. The clouds of Neptune are composed mostly of ----

   A. methane   B. hydrogen sulphide

   C. ammonia   D. All of the above

9. The distance of planet Neptune from Sun is ----

   A. 18 AU   B. 30 AU

   C. 52 AU   D. 70AU

10. Wind speeds on Neptune can reach supersonic speeds

   A. True   B. False

11. The equatorial diameter of Neptune is ----

   A. 29,528 km   B. 49,528 km

   C. 79,528 km   D. 99,528 km

12. The mass of Neptune is ----- times than that of Earth.

   A. 5   B. 11

   C. 17   D. 38

13. Neptune has ----- moons

   A. 7   B. 14

   C. 21   D. 32

14. Planet Neptune was discovered by ----

   A. Urbain Le Verrier &   B. Galileo
      Johann Galle

   C. Aryabhata   D. Copernicus

15   The surface temperature on Neptune is ----

    A.   68 deg C   B.   -105 deg C

    C.   -201 deg C   D.   -298 deg C

16.   Which is the only planet in our solar system not visible to the naked eye

    A.   Uranus   B.   Jupiter

    C.   Mercury   D.   Neptune

17.   The only spacecraft to have visited Neptune very close?

    A.   Pioneer   B.   Cassini

    C.   Voyager-2   D.   Apollo-8

18.   How many times Neptune is wider than our Earth?

    A.   2   B.   4

    C.   6   D.   8

19.   Which is the windiest planet in our solar system?

    A.   Saturn   B.   Neptune

    C.   Jupiter   D.   Uranus

20.   Triton, the largest of Neptune's moons displays retrograde revolution

    A.   True   B.   False

17. The Earth's Moon

17.1 The Earth's Moon

Quiz-26

1. Which is the natural satellite of Earth?
   A. The Sun
   B. The Moon
   C. Comet
   D. Asteroid

2. The average distance of the Moon from Earth?
   A. 0.5 light seconds
   B. 1.0 light seconds
   C. 1.28 light seconds
   D. 2.1 light seconds

3. What is the size of the moon compared to Earth?
   A. 10.4%
   B. 19.8%
   C. 27.2%
   D. 45.4%

4. The volume of Moon is about --- of the earth's volume
   A. 2%
   B. 8%
   C. 16%
   D. 21%

5. Earth's moon is the ---- moon in the solar system.
   A. 2nd largest
   B. 5th largest
   C. Largest
   D. Smallest

6. The moon's mass is ----
   A. 0.2% of Earth mass
   B. 0.6% of Earth mass
   C. 1.2% of Earth mass
   D. 2.8% of Earth mass

7. How many American astronauts have explored the lunar surface?
   A. 8
   B. 12
   C. 16
   D. 20

8. The average distance from the Moon to the Earth?

   A. 384,400 miles
   B. 384,400 km
   C. 150,000 miles
   D. 150,000 km

9. The moon's density is about ---- of Earth's density

   A. 30%
   B. 40%
   C. 50%
   D. 60%

10. A person who can jump up 10 feet on Earth would be able to jump almost 60 feet on the moon.

    A. True
    B. False

11. The Earth weighs --- times more than the moon.

    A. 8
    B. 21
    C. 41
    D. 81

12. The average surface temperature of the Moon during the day is ----

    A. 44°C
    B. 78°C
    C. 127°C
    D. 205°C

13. At any time from Earth, what percentage of the surface of the Moon we can see

    A. 30 %
    B. 50%
    C. 75 %
    D. 100%

14. The mass of a person on Earth is 60 kg. What is the mass of that person on Moon?

    A. 10 kg
    B. 20 kg
    C. 40 kg
    D. 60 kg

15. If your weight on Earth is 60 kg. What will be your weight on Moon?

    A. 10 kg
    B. 40 kg
    C. 60 kg
    D. 90 kg

16. The mean orbital velocity of the moon is ----

    A. 0.25 km/s
    B. 0.52 km/s
    C. 1.02 km/s
    D. 1.56 km/s

17. Which is the tallest mountain on the Moon, it is just over half the height of Mt Everest?

    A. Mons Moro
    B. Mons Pico
    C. Mons Piton
    D. Mons Huygens

18. The acceleration due to gravity on the surface of the moon is ...

    A. $1.624 \, m/s^2$
    B. $2.624 \, m/s^2$
    C. $3.624 \, m/s^2$
    D. $9.81 \, m/s^2$

19. When a full moon coincides with perigee, we get a ...

    A. Lunar eclipse
    B. Supermoon
    C. Half-moon
    D. Crescent moon

20. During a supermoon, the moon appears --- than usual

    A. 14 percent larger and 30 percent brighter
    B. 30 percent larger and 14 percent brighter
    C. 5 percent larger and 20 percent brighter
    D. 20 percent larger and 5 percent brighter

Quiz-27

1. How many hours make one day on moon?

   A. 122.6   B. 346.8

   C. 655.7   D. 986.8

2. What is a blue moon?

   A. The first of two full Moons that appear during the same month

   B. The second of two full Moons that appear during the same month

   C. The first of two full Moons that appear during the same year

   D. The second of two full Moons that appear during the same year

3. A supermoon occurs about every ----

   A. 100 days   B. 212 days

   C. 414 days   D. 618 days

4. A day on the Moon is ---- Earth days

   A. 8.26   B. 19.16

   C. 27.32   D. 46.87

5. The Moon appears to shine because of what?

   A. Moon generates continuous hot gases

   B. Sunlight is reflected from the Moon's surface

   C. Its proximity from Earth

   D. Tidal energy

6. The side that we can see from Earth is called the near side while the other side is

   A. Another side   B. Hidden side

   C. Dark side   D. Bright side

7. From Earth, both the Sun and the Moon look about the same size. This is because
   A. Both Sun and Moon are of the same size
   B. The Moon is 400 times smaller than the Sun, but also 400 times closer to Earth.
   C. The Moon is 800 times smaller than the Sun
   D. The Moon is 800 times smaller than the Sun, but also 800 times closer to Earth.

8. The rise and fall of the tides on Earth are caused by the ---
   A. Earth
   B. Moon
   C. Sun
   D. None of the above

9. The Earth's Moon is the ---- satellite in the solar system
   A. Second densest
   B. Third densest
   C. Densest
   D. Least dense

10. The Moon always shows Earth the same face
    A. True
    B. False

11. We cannot hear any sound on moon, this is because of ----
    A. Lack of atmosphere
    B. Lack of Oxygen
    C. Less gravity on moon
    D. It is not a planet

12. The moon atmosphere is made up of
    A. Oxygen
    B. Nitrogen
    C. Hydrogen and Helium
    D. Nothing

13. How does erosion occur on moon?
    A. Wind shear
    B. High temperature
    C. Earthquakes
    D. There is no erosion on moon

14. The diameter of Earth's Moon is just smaller than -----
and just bigger than -----, the other two moons of solar
system
  A. Titania, Callisto   B. Europa, Io
  C. Io, Europa   D. Triton, Io

15. What is the direction of Moon's orbit about earth?
  A. North to South   B. East to West
  C. South to North   D. Same as Earth's rotation

16. When a second full Moon occurs during a calendar
month, it is called?
  A. Big Moon   B. Second Moon
  C. Red Moon   D. Blue Moon

17. Early astronomers used to call large dark spots on the
Moon as ---
  A. Selena   B. Maria
  C. Luna   D. Venus

18. How does the Moon stay on orbit?
  A. Because of the Earth's gravity
  B. Because of the Sun's gravity.
  C. Because of strong magnetic field
  D. Because of the large internal energy

19. How long is the Moon's synodic period?
  A. 8 days   B. 19 days
  C. 29.5 days   D. 4 weeks

20. Which of the following moons in solar system is
smaller than Earth's moon
  A. Ganymede   B. Titan
  C. Europa   D. Io

17.2 Phases of the Moon
Quiz-28

Following questions (1 to 8) are with respect to the figure shown below:

1. The phase of the moon at location 'A' is called ---
   A. Full Moon   B. First Quarter
   C. New Moon   D. Second Quarter

2. The phase of the moon at location 'B' is called ---
   A. Waxing Crescent   B. Waning Crescent
   C. Waxing Gibbous   D. Waning Gibbous

3. The phase of the moon at location 'C' is called
   A. Full moon   B. First quarter
   C. Third quarter   D. New moon

4. The phase of the moon at location 'D' is called ......

    A. Waning Gibbous   B. Waxing Gibbous

    C. Waxing Crescent   D. Waning Crescent

5. The phase of the moon at location 'E' is called ......

    A. New moon   B. Full moon

    C. Bright moon   D. Dark moon

6. The phase of the moon at location 'F' is called ......

    A. Waxing Crescent   B. Waning Crescent

    C. Waxing Gibbous   D. Waning Gibbous

7. The phase of the moon at location 'G' is called ......

    A. First Quarter   B. Second Quarter

    C. Third Quarter   D. Fourth Quarter

8. The phase of the moon at location 'H' is called ---

    A. Waning Crescent   B. Waxing Crescent

    C. Waxing Gibbous   D. Waning Gibbous

9. How much of the Moon is continuously lit up?

    A. 10%   B. 25%

    C. 50%   D. 100%

10. How often do the phases of the Moon cycle repeat?

    A. Around once an hour   B. Every 24 hours

    C. Around once a week   D. Once a month

11. What is the phase of the Moon when the Moon sits between the Sun and the Earth?

A. Crescent Moon
B. Quarter Moon
C. Full Moon
D. New Moon

12. What is the phase of the Moon when 100% of the Moon is lit up?

A. New moon
B. Full moon
C. Half-moon
D. Bright moon

13. The moon is said to be waning when any portion of the moon's right half is not visible or when the illuminated sliver is on the left

A. True
B. False

14. What do you call a phase of the Moon when less than half of the Moon is lit up?

A. Gibbous moon
B. Quarter Moon
C. Crescent Moon
D. Partial Moon

15. What is the phase of the Moon when more than half of the Moon is lit up?

A. Gibbous moon
B. Crescent Moon
C. Quarter Moon
D. Partial Moon

16. The waning crescent will grow smaller and smaller every day, until the Moon looks like the ---

A. First quarter
B. Second quarter
C. New Moon
D. Full Moon

17. What is the period when you see more and more of the Moon each night?

   A. Phasing moon
   B. Diminishing moon
   C. Waning Moon
   D. Waxing moon

18. If exactly half of the Moon is lit up, it is called "Crescent Moon"

   A. True
   B. False

19. The correct order of different phases of moon is – "New Moon, Waxing Crescent, First Quarter, Waxing Gibbous"

   A. True
   B. False

20. The moon is waxing when the illuminated sliver is on the right.

   A. True
   B. False

17.3 The Moon Mission

Quiz-29

1. In which year did the Soviet Union land an unmanned craft on the moon?

   A. 1958   B. 1966

   C. 1976   D. 1982

2. The Apollo 11 mission was the first craft to land on the moon.

   A. True

   B. False

3. The first successful landing of an unmanned spacecraft on the surface of the Moon was ----

   A. Apollo 11   B. Apollo 1

   C. Sputnik 1   D. Luna - 2

4. In Apollo 11 mission team, which astronauts didn't walk on the moon?

   A. Michael Collins   B. Neil Armstrong

   C. Buzz Aldrin   D. Yuri Gagarin

5. How many Russians have landed on Moon?

   A. 0   B. 2

   C. 4   D. 6

6. On which date, the first human-made object, Luna-2 landed at the surface of the Moon?

   A. 12 April 1956   B. 13 September 1959

   C. 20 July 1962   D. 14 October 1971

7. What was the name of the mission that resulted in the first manned moon landing?

   A. Soyuz-1   B. Apollo 13

   C. Apollo 11   D. Vostok-2

8. On which date, the first human landed at the surface of the Moon?

   A. 12 April 1956   B. 13 September, 1959

   C. 20 July, 1969   D. 14 October 1971

9. The first man to land on moon?

   A. Neil Armstrong   B. Buzz Aldrin

   C. Michael Collins   D. Yuri Gagarin

10. Which rocket was used to launch Apollo-11?

    A. Saturn-5   B. Vostok-I

    C. Ariane-II   D. PSLV

11. What is featured on the official Apollo 11 emblem?

    A. American flag   B. Earth logo

    C. Astronauts in Apollo 11   D. Bald Eagle on the moon

12. What sample of mineral was brought by astronauts of Apollo-11 back to Earth?

    A. Titanium   B. Armacolite

    C. Niobium   D. Plutonium

13. Other than Neil Armstrong and Buzz Aldrin, who was the third member in the Apollo 11 mission?

    A. Michael Collins   B. Alan Shepard

    C. Yuri Gagarin   D. James Lovell

14. How long it took for Apollo 11 from blast-off to go to the moon and touchdown back on Earth?

 A. 4 days   B. 6 days

 C. 8 days   D. 10 days

15. The "Blue Marble" photograph of Earth was taken during

 A. Apollo 8 mission   B. Apollo 11 mission

 C. Apollo 13 mission   D. Apollo 17 mission

16. What was the name of the ship that landed on the Moon

 A. Eagle   B. Falcon

 C. Bird   D. Luna

17. Why do footprints ever stay on Moon?

 A. The surface is highly rocky

 B. There are no people there

 C. There is no atmosphere

 D. None of these

18. Which president of the USA initiated and encourage the landing of man on the Moon?

 A. John F. Kennedy   B. Richard Nixon

 C. George Bush   D. None

19. Which of the following astronauts was not a part of the lunar mission team?

 A. Neil Armstrong   B. Buzz Aldrin

 C. Michael Collins   D. Allan Shepard

20. In which ocean did the returning Columbia module splash down?

 A. Indian ocean   B. Pacific Ocean

 C. Atlantic Ocean   D. Caspian Sea

Quiz-30

1. The last Apollo mission was in ----
   A. 1962
   B. 1968
   C. 1972
   D. 1974

2. Which is the only portion of the Apollo 11 spacecraft returned back to Earth?
   A. Service module
   B. Command module
   C. Lunar module
   D. Middle portion

3. Who was president of the U.S. at the time of the moon landing?
   A. Lyndon B. Johnson
   B. Richard Nixon
   C. George Bush
   D. John F Kennedy

4. The general area in which the Eagle landed was called ----
   A. Florida state
   B. Tycho crater
   C. Arctic Ocean
   D. The Sea of Tranquility

5. How many total Apollo manned moon missions have taken place since 1969?
   A. 4
   B. 5
   C. 6
   D. 7

6. Which Apollo mission could not land on Moon?
   A. Apollo 11
   B. Apollo 12
   C. Apollo 13
   D. Apollo 14

7. That's one small step for (a) man. One giant leap for mankind." Who spoke these words on moon?
   A. Neil Armstrong
   B. Buzz Aldrin
   C. Michael Collins
   D. Allan Shepard

8. What was the name of the module which ultimately brought the astronauts back to Earth during the lunar landing mission in July 1969

A. Command Module, "Columbia"
B. Command Module, "Discovery"
C. Command Module, "Antares"
D. Command Module, "Challenger"

9. Which is the only ill-fated Apollo mission, that had to abort its moon landing

A. Apollo 11
B. Apollo 12
C. Apollo 13
D. Apollo 14

10. In which of the following Apollo mission, the cabin fire killed the entire crew during a prelaunch test

A. Apollo-1
B. Apollo-5
C. Apollo-8
D. Apollo-13

11. When did the U.S. end its lunar flights?

A. 1970
B. 1971
C. 1972
D. 1974

12. Which was the last Apollo mission?

A. Apollo 12
B. Apollo 14
C. Apollo 17
D. Apollo 19

13. Footprints stay on the Moon because ----

A. No human on moon to disturb them
B. The Moon has no atmosphere
C. Solid rock pattern on moon
D. None of these

14. Human Moon landings missions were between the years
    A. 1963-1966   B. 1966-1969
    C. 1969–1972   D. 1972-1975

15. How long it took from blast-off from Earth to touchdown on Moon and back on Earth?
    A. 2 days   B. 4 days
    C. 6 days   D. 8 days

16. Which craft was the first to reach the surface of the moon?
    A. Luna 1   B. Luna 2
    C. Apollo 1   D. Apollo 10

17. What was the name of the Indian lunar mission launched on 22 July 2019
    A. Gaganyan-1   B. Chandrayan-1
    C. Chandrayan-2   D. Mission moon

18. Which launch vehicle was used to launch Chandrayan-2
    A. PSLV Mk-II   B. GSLV Mk-II
    C. PSLV Mk-III   D. PSLV Mk-IV

19. What was the name of the lander for mission Chandrayan-2 designed for a soft landing on moon
    A. Pragyan   B. Vikram
    C. Orbiter   D. Rover

20. The name of the rover in mission Chandrayan-2?
    A. Bharat   B. Vikram
    C. Orbiter   D. Pragyan

18. Other Moons of Solar System

126

Quiz-31

1. Which terrestrial planet has only one moon?

   A. Earth
   B. Venus
   C. Mercury
   D. All of the above

2. Moons are also known as ----

   A. Asteroids
   B. Meteorites
   C. Natural satellites
   D. Small Planets

3. The largest moon of our solar system?

   A. Ganymede
   B. Titan
   C. Earth's moon
   D. Io

4. The second largest moon of our solar system?

   A. Ganymede
   B. Titan
   C. Earth's moon
   D. Io

5. The moon 'Titan' is larger than the planet Mercury?

   A. True
   B. False

6. Moons of which planet are named after great literature

   A. Saturn
   B. Jupiter
   C. Uranus
   D. Neptune

7. Which of the following planets do not have any moon?

   A. Venus and Mercury
   B. Mercury and Mars
   C. Mars and Neptune
   D. Mercury and Uranus

8. Which planet in our solar system has the smallest moon?

  A. Mercury   B. Venus

  C. Earth   D. Mars

9. Which planet has the biggest moon in solar system?

  A. Earth   B. Uranus

  C. Jupiter   D. Saturn

10. Triton is a retrograde moon

  A. True   B. False

11. Most heavily cratered moon in our solar system?

  A. Ganymede   B. Titan

  C. Callisto   D. Io

12. Saturn has 82 moons.

  A. True   B. False

13. Number of moons of Jupiter?

  A. 24   B. 48

  C. 79   D. 87

14. Third largest moon in solar system?

  A. Ganymede   B. Titan

  C. Callisto   D. Io

15 Fourth largest moon in solar system?

  A. Earth's moon B. Titan

  C. Callisto   D. Io

16. The fifth-largest moon in the solar system?

   A. Earth's Moon   B. Titan

   C. Callisto   D. Io

17. The biggest moon of Uranus?

   A. Miranda   B. Titania

   C. Ariel   D. Oberon

18. The biggest moon of Neptune?

   A. Naiad   B. Thalassa

   C. Galatea   D. Triton

19. Neptune has how many moons?

   A. 2   B. 6

   C. 9   D. 14

20. Uranus has how many moons?

   A. 7   B. 17

   C. 27   D. 37

19. Dwarf Planets

Quiz-32

1. Dwarf planets are different from large planets because,

   A. Dwarf planets do not orbit the Sun

   B. Dwarf planets orbit only Gas giants

   C. Dwarf planets orbit only terrestrial planets

   D. Dwarf planets failed to clear their neighborhood

2. Eris is the largest dwarf planet?

   A. True   B. False

3. How many officially classified dwarf planets are there in our solar system?

   A. 2   B. 3

   C. 4   D. 5

4. The dwarf planet 'Ceres' is located inside the asteroid belt between the orbits of Mars and Jupiter?

   A. True   B. False

5. Pluto was reclassified as dwarf planet in 2006

   A. True   B. false

6. Which is the smallest dwarf planet?

   A. Eris   B. Ceres

   C. Pluto   D. Haumea

7. In which year the International Astronomical Union (IAU) defined "dwarf planets

   A. 1998   B. 2002

   C. 2006   D. 2009

8. The dwarf planet farthest from the Sun?

   A. Ceres B. Eris

   C. Pluto D. Haumea

9. The most massive dwarf planet?

   A. Eris B. Makemake

   C. Pluto D. Haumea

10. Except Ceres, all other dwarf planets are located near the

    A. Kuiper belt B. Asteroid belt

    C. Sun D. Earth's orbit

11. What do we call the celestial objects in the region outside the planet Neptune?

    A. Blackhole B. Asteroid belt

    C. Kuiper belt D. Outermost belt

12. Eris is located beyond the orbit of Neptune and the Kuiper belt in a region known as the Scattered disc

    A. True B. False

13. The diameter of the largest dwarf planet, Eris is ----

    A. $1/3^{rd}$ Earth's moon B. $1/4^{th}$ Earth's moon

    C. $2/3^{rd}$ Earth's moon D. Same as Earth's moon

14 The dwarf planet Ceres is closest to the Sun?

    A. True B. False

15. This dwarf planet was once considered to become the tenth planet of the solar system

   A. Makemake   B. Ceres

   C. Haumea   D. Eris

16. The dwarf planet second closest to the Sun?

   A. Makemake   B. Ceres

   C. Haumea   D. Pluto

17. The number of moons of Pluto?

   A. 0   B. 2

   C. 3   D. 5

18. The largest moon of Pluto?

   A. Charon   B. Kerberos

   C. Hydra   D. Nix

19. This dwarf planet does not have its own moon?

   A. Ceres   B. Eris

   C. Haumea   D. Pluto

20. Which is the least spherical of all dwarf planets?

   A. Haumea   B. Eris

   C. Charon   D. Pluto

20. Solar Eclipse

Quiz-33

1. What is the Solar Eclipse?

   A. When the moon comes in between Earth and Sun

   B. When Earth comes in between Moon and Sun

   C. When Sun comes in between Earth and Moon

   D. When Sun rays do not reach Earth

2. Sometimes we see the annular solar eclipse and not a total solar eclipse. This is because ...

   A. the Moon is much nearer in its orbit than usual

   B. the Moon is farther away in its orbit than usual

   C. the Moon travels slower in its orbit than usual

   D. the Moon travels faster in its orbit than usual

3. In this cycle, we see the same pattern of solar eclipse repeating every 18 years 11 days, and 8 hours.

   A. Solar cycle   B. Lunar cycle

   C. Saros cycle   D. Galactic cycle

4. A diamond ring occurs in 'Total Solar eclipse'

   A. True   B. False

5. What is the minimum number of solar eclipses that can occur during a calendar year?

   A. 0   B. 1

   C. 2   D. 3

6. After how many years the same total solar eclipse will occur at the same place on earth?

   A. 1 year   B. 18 years, 6months

   C. 375 years   D. Not possible

7. Only partial solar eclipses can be observed from the North and South Poles

   A. True   B. False

8. The longest possible duration of a total solar eclipse?

   A. 5 minutes, 12 seconds   B. 7 minutes, 32 seconds

   C. 8 minutes, 52 seconds   D. 9 minutes, 24 seconds

9. What is the maximum number of solar eclipses that can occur during a calendar year?

   A. 2   B. 3

   C. 4   D. 5

10. Solar eclipses always occur on new moon

    A. True   B. False

11. In which type of eclipse, the moon comes in between the Sun and the Earth?

    A. Solar eclipse   B. Lunar eclipse

12. The shadow during a solar eclipse, which keeps getting smaller as it goes away from Sun is called ----

    A. Umbra   B. Penumbra

    C. Total shadow   D. Dark shadow

13. The shadow during a solar eclipse, which keeps getting larger as it goes away from the Sun is called ----

    A. Umbra   Penumbra

    C. Total shadow   Dark shadow

14. What is the maximum number of solar eclipses (partial, annular, or total) per year

    A. 1   B. 3

    C. 5   D. 7

15. The correct alignment during a solar eclipse?
    A. Sun, Moon, Earth   B. Sun, Earth, Moon
    C. Moon, Sun, Earth   D. None of these

16. What type of solar eclipse is this?
    A. Total solar eclipse
    B. Annular solar eclipse
    C. Partial solar eclipse
    D. None of these

17. What type of solar eclipse is this?
    A. Total solar eclipse
    B. Annular solar eclipse
    C. Partial solar eclipse
    D. None of these

18. What type of solar eclipses cannot be seen from the North and South Poles
    A. Total solar eclipse   B. Partial solar eclipse
    C. Annular solar eclipse D. None of these

19. The maximum possible duration for an annular solar eclipse is ----
    A. 4 minutes and 24 seconds
    B. 7 minutes and 18 seconds
    C. 12 minutes and 29 seconds
    D. 18 minutes and 32 seconds

20. What is the maximum width of the path of totality during Solar Eclipse?
    A. 168 km   B. 198 km
    C. 232 km   D. 269 km

21. Lunar Eclipse

Quiz-34

1. When Lunar Eclipse occur?

   A. When Sun is between Earth and Moon

   B. When Earth is between Sun and Moon

   C. When Moon is between Earth and Sun

   D. When Earth is between Sun and other celestial bodies

2. A lunar eclipse takes place when

   A. Earth passes through Sun's shadow

   B. The moon passes through the sun's shadow

   C. The moon passes through the earth's shadow

   D. The moon passes through the sun's shadow

3. The alignment of the Earth, Sun, and Moon is called ---

   A. Syzygy   B. Plane

   C. Linear   D. Ysyzyg

4. How many maximum lunar eclipses can occur in a calendar year?

   A. 1   B. 3

   C. 5   D. 7

5. The duration of a lunar eclipse is ----

   A. Shorter than a solar eclipse

   B. Longer than a solar eclipse

   C. Almost the same as a solar eclipse

   D. Depends upon the totality of the solar eclipse

6. A solar eclipse happens during the Full Moon and the lunar eclipse happens during a New Moon

   A. True   B. False

7. On average, in how many years, a total lunar eclipse can be seen from any given location?

   A. 1 year   B. 2.5 years
   C. 4.5 years   D. 10 years

8. Which position of the Sun, Earth, and Moon causes the Lunar eclipse?

   A.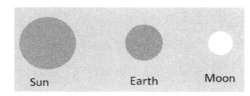

   B.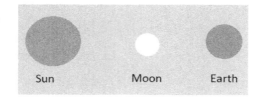

9. Earth's shadow can be divided into two distinctive parts: the umbra and penumbra. The umbra is darker than the penumbra.

   A. True   B. False

10. A total lunar eclipse can last up to nearly 2 hours, while a total solar eclipse lasts only up to a few minutes at any given place

    A. True   B. False

11. During a lunar eclipse, the visible red color is because of:

A. Dust particles in space

B. Dust in the moon's atmosphere

C. Sunlight refracted by Earth's atmosphere

D. Dust in Sun's atmosphere

12. During a total lunar eclipse, an observer on the moon would see,

A. Shining ring of Sun's atmosphere

B. Shining ring of Earth's atmosphere

C. Corona of the sun

D. Complete darkness

13. Eclipses do not occur every month because the orbit of the moon is

A. Elliptical

B. Circular

C. Linear

D. Tilted

14. Lunar eclipse can be seen when there is

A. Crescent moon

B. new moon

C. First quarter

D. Full moon

15. During a total lunar eclipse, a person on Earth would see

A. Moon turning a black color

B. Moon turning a white color

C. Moon turning a red color

D. None of these

16. During a total lunar eclipse, the moon is in Earth's

A. Umbra
B. Penumbra
C. Shadow
D. Exosphere

17. The correct alignment during a total lunar eclipse is

A. Sun, Moon, Earth
B. Sun, Earth, Moon
C. Earth, Sun, Moon
D. None of the above

18. The moon's orbit is tilted about --- degrees relative to Earth's orbit around the Sun

A. 10.5
B. 18.6
C. 29.5
D. 36.9

19. The darkest part of the moon's shadow is called the

A. Umbra
B. Penumbra
C. Shadow
D. Dark spots

20. The Earth's moon in a total lunar eclipse is also called a

A. Black moon
B. Blood moon
C. Dark moon
D. Brown moon

22. Asteroids & Meteorites

Quiz-35

1. Small bodies of rock or metal orbiting the Sun are called

   A. Rocky planets
   B. Meteoroids
   C. Asteroids
   D. Comets

2. Which asteroid was discovered first?

   A. Ceres
   B. Vesta
   C. Ida
   D. Eros

3. Who discovered the first asteroid Ceres?

   A. Giuseppe Piazzi
   B. William Hershel
   C. Galileo Galilei
   D. Copernicus

4. When a meteoroid enters the Earth's atmosphere and vaporizes and looks like a shooting star are called ---

   A. A meteor
   B. An asteroid
   C. A comet
   D. A Meteoroid

5. A meteoroid entering Earth's atmosphere is heated by friction

   A. True
   B. False

6. Astronomer William Herschel first coined the word asteroid, which means ----

   A. Rock like
   B. Star like
   C. Shining
   D. Ice like

7. The main asteroid belt lies between the orbits of ----

   A. Earth and Mars.
   B. Saturn and Jupiter
   C. Venus and Earth
   D. Mars and Jupiter

8. Meteorites are of three types: stony, stony-iron, or iron.

   A. True   B. False

9. A small particle from a comet/asteroid orbiting the Sun is

   A. Meteorite   B. Meteoroid

   C. Asteroid   D. Comet

10. Asteroids are leftovers of the early Solar System

   A. True   B. False

11. Every day, Earth is bombarded with more than 100 tons of dust and sand-sized particles

   A. True   B. False

12. No asteroid has a satellite of its own

   A. True   B. False

13. The name given to asteroid groups formed after collision and sharing similar composition are called?

   A. Trojan families   B. Piazzi families

   C. Hirayama families   D. Galilean families

14. Which asteroids group share Jupiter's orbit?

   A. Piazzi asteroids   B. Cassini asteroids

   C. Trojan asteroids   D. None of the above

15 A meteoroid that survives its passage through the Earth's atmosphere and lands upon the Earth's surface is called

   A. Meteorite   B. Comet

   C. Meteoroid   D. Asteroid

16. What is the size of the smallest asteroid 2015 TC25?

    A. 2 m wide
    B. 5 m wide
    C. 10 m wide
    D. 50m wide

17. In the asteroid belt, the area free of asteroids are called

    A. Piazzi's gaps
    B. Kirkwood's gaps
    C. Cassini gaps
    D. Hershel gaps

18. The first asteroid Ceres was named after which Roman goddess?

    A. Goddess of harvest
    B. Goddess of wealth
    C. Goddess of love
    D. Goddess of peace

19. Which celestial object is both the largest of the asteroids and the only dwarf planet inside Neptune's orbit

    A. Pallas
    B. Vesta
    C. Ceres
    D. Hygiea

20. Some asteroids are blown-out comets

    A. True
    B. False

23. Comets

Quiz-36

1. An irregularly shaped body composed mostly of a mixture of water ice, dust, carbon, and silicon-based compounds with a glowing tail is called?

   A. Asteroid
   B. Meteorite
   C. Comet
   D. Dwarf planet

2. Comets originating from outside the solar system called?

   A. Napier belt
   B. Oort cloud
   C. Asteroid belt
   D. Cassini space

3. Halley's Comet was named after English astronomer ---

   A. Edmond Halley
   B. Robert Halley
   C. William Halley
   D. Chris Halley

4. Halley's Comet was last seen in 1986

   A. True
   B. False

5. Early days, people used to think by seeing a comet?

   A. Disaster
   B. Disease
   C. Death
   D. All above

6. The bright glow around the head of a comet is called

   A. Crown
   B. Coma
   C. Body
   D. Tail

7. The famous comet, seen from Earth once in 75 years?

   A. Halley's Comet
   B. Shoemaker Levy-9
   C. Hale-Bopp
   D. Comet Encke

8. The distinct part of a comet?

   A. Nucleus   B. Tail

   C. Coma   D. All of the above

9. The tail extends from the comet and points ----

   A. Towards the Sun   B. Away from the Sun

   C. Towards the Earth   D. Away from Earth

10. You can't see a comet without a telescope

   A. True   B. False

11. What do we call the solid core of a comet?

   A. Tail   B. Coma

   C. Nucleus   D. Interior part

12. A comet generally has ----

   A. One type of tail   B. Two types of tail

   C. Three types of tail   D. Four types of tail

13. Comets are often called "Dirty snowballs"?

   A. True   B. False

14. What is the size of the nuclei of most comets?

   A. 414 km   B. 1,414 km

   C. 2,414 km   D. 3,414 km

15 How many tails does a comet have?

   A. No tails   B. One

   C. 2, an ion and dust tail   D. More than 10 tails

16. Which comet has the shortest known orbital period?

    A. Comet Halley
    B. Comet Encke
    C. Shoemaker Levy-9
    D. Comet Mrkos

17. Name the comet that smashed into Jupiter in 1994?

    A. Hale-Bopp
    B. Shoemaker Levy-9
    C. Halley's Comet
    D. None of the above

18. Which famous comet will be seen in 2061?

    A. Comet Halley
    B. Comet Encke
    C. Shoemaker Levy-9
    D. Comet Bennett

19. The first person to predict the return of a comet?

    A. John Kepler
    B. Nicolaus Copernicus
    C. Galileo Galilei
    D. Edmond Halley

20. What was the brightest comet in the 20th Century?

    A. Comet Ikeya-Seki
    B. Comet Halley
    C. Comet Encke
    D. Comet Shoemaker Levy-9

24. Solar System-Mixed Quiz

Quiz-37

1. Smallest planet of the solar system?

   A. Mars B. Mercury

   C. Venus D. Uranus

2. The largest planet of the solar system?

   A. Uranus B. Saturn

   C. Jupiter D. Earth

3. The planet nearest to Sun?

   A. Mercury B. Mars

   C. Venus D. Earth

4. The planet farthest from Sun?

   A. Mercury B. Neptune

   C. Venus D. Earth

5. The planet with a spectacular ring system?

   A. Mars B. Saturn

   C. Jupiter D. Uranus

6. The planet having maximum number of moons?

   A. Jupiter B. Saturn

   C. Uranus D. Earth

7. The planet having no moon?

    A. Mars   B. Earth

    C. Neptune   D. Mercury

8. This planet has only one moon?

    A. Uranus   B. Jupiter

    C. Earth   D. Saturn

9. Total number of planets in our solar system?

    A. 6   B. 7

    C. 8   D. 9

10. A day on planet Venus is longer than a year

    A. True   B. False

11. Number of recognized dwarf planets in our solar system?

    A. 1   B. 2

    C. 3   D. 5

12. How many stars in our solar system?

    A. 0   B. 1

    C. 3   D. 4

13. Venus is the brightest planet in our Solar system.

    A. True   B. False

14. Who discovered Uranus?

    A. William Herschel   B. Galileo Galilei

    C. Copernicus   D. Isaac Newton

15 Which planet has the maximum orbital velocity?

A. Mercury B. Uranus

C. Earth D. Jupiter

16. Which planet has the minimum orbital velocity?

A. Venus B. Uranus

C. Jupiter D. Neptune

17. Least dense planet of our solar system?

A. Neptune B. Saturn

C. Jupiter D. Uranus

18. Densest planet of the solar system?

A. Mars B. Jupiter

C. Neptune D. Earth

19. Jupiter, Saturn, Uranus and Neptune are called ----

A. Inner planets B. Big planets

C. Terrestrial planets D. Gas giants

20. Mercury, Venus, Earth, Mars are called ----

A. Minor planets B. Outer planets

C. Terrestrial planets D. Gas giants

Quiz-38

1. The hottest planet in our solar system?

   A. Earth   B. Mercury

   C. Saturn   D. Venus

2. Coldest planet in our solar system?

   A. Neptune   B. Uranus

   C. Saturn   D. Venus

3. The windiest planet in the solar system?

   A. Earth   B. Uranus

   C. Mars   D. Neptune

4. The red planet in our solar system?

   A. Neptune   B. Venus

   C. Mars   D. Saturn

5. Jupiter is a terrestrial planet?

   A. True   B. False

6. What is the name of the largest moon of Saturn?

   A. Janus   B. Rhea

   C. Mimas   D. Titan

7. The largest moon in our solar system?

   A. Oberon   B. Ganymede

   C. Moon   D. Titan

8. Planet Venus has no natural satellites?

    A. True   B. False

9. What is the Surface temperature of Sun?

    A. 2,777 K   B. 5,777 K

    C. 10,777 K   D. 20,777 K

10. The sunlight takes --- to travel from the Sun to Neptune

    A. 2 hours   B. 3 hours

    C. 4 hours   D. 5 hours

11. The sun's energy comes from ---- fusion reactions

    A. Uranium   B. Helium

    C. Carbon   D. Hydrogen

12. Since its discovery, how many orbits Neptune has completed around Sun?

    A. 0   A. 1

    C. 2   D. 3

13. Which is the only moon in the solar system that circles its planet in the opposite direction to the planet's rotation

    A. Triton   B. Atlas

    C. Titan   D. Rhea

14. What gas is the main component of Mars atmosphere?

    A. Sulphur   B. Oxygen

    C. Carbon Dioxide   D. Nitrogen

15. What do we call the path in the sky that the sun appears to traverse over the course of a year?

    A. Elliptic   B. Circular

    C. Ecliptic   D. Spiral

16. What percentage of the Sun's mass has been converted to energy?

   A.   50%   B.   1%

   C.   2%   D.   0.001%

17. In our solar system, which dwarf planet has a moon with a mass closest to its own?

   A.   Eris   B.   Makemake

   C.   Haumea   D.   Pluto

18. What is a sunspot?

   A.   Areas of increased   B.   Areas of reduced
        surface temperature   surface temperature

   C.   Areas of the high   D.   Areas of the nuclear
        gravitated field   explosion

19. Most of the asteroids are located between which planets?

   A.   Jupiter and Saturn   B.   Mars and Jupiter

   C.   Earth and Mars   D.   Mars and Venus

20. How many moons does Jupiter has?

   A.   11   B.   24

   C.   44   D.   79

Quiz-39

1. What are "cool" areas on the surface of the Sun called?

    A. Dusty Spots B. Sun Spots

    C. Fire Spots D. Ice Spots

2. How was the planet Neptune discovered?

    A. Telescope from ground B. Telescope from Space

    C. Mathematical calculations D. None of the above

3. The Sun rotates on its axis once in about ---- days.

    A. 11 B. 19

    C. 27 D. 36

4. A day on the Moon is ---- Earth days

    A. 27.32 B. 46.87

    C. 8.26 D. 1

5. Which is the hottest layer of the sun?

    A. Corona B. Chromosphere

    C. Photosphere D. None

6. The Sun is a loner, while most of the stars have companions.

    A. True B. False

7. Who discovered the planet Neptune?

    A. William Herschel B. Copernicus

    C. Urbain Le Verrier D. Isaac Newton

8. Out of eight planets, six planets while revolving around Sun in an anti-clockwise direction also rotate anti-clockwise on their axis. Which two planets do not rotate anti-clockwise on their axis while revolving around Sun?

    A. Venus and Uranus   B. Mars and Jupiter

    C. Venus and Neptune   D. Neptune and Uranus

9. Which direction the Sun rotates on its own axis?

    A. Clockwise   B. Anti-clockwise

    C. Sun does not rotate   D. None of the above

10. The side that we can see from Earth is called the near side while the other side is

    A. Far side   B. Dark side

    C. Hidden side   D. Bright side

11. Which of the following planets do not have any moon?

    A. Mercury and Mars   B. Mars and Neptune

    C. Venus and Mercury   D. Mercury and Uranus

12. Which planet has the shortest day?

    A. Mercury   B. Jupiter

    C. Saturn   D. Venus

13. Which planet has the longest day?

    A. Mercury   B. Jupiter

    C. Saturn   D. Venus

14. Which planet takes minimum time to orbit the Sun?

    A. Mercury   B. Jupiter

    C. Saturn   D. Venus

15. Which planet takes maximum time to orbit the Sun?

    A. Uranus   B. Jupiter

    C. Saturn   D. Neptune

16. Uranus extreme tilt is supposed to be due to ----

    A. Very high gravity   B. Strong solar storm

    C. A collision with a planet soon after its formation   D. Strong magnetic field

17. The first planet to be discovered with a telescope was

    A. Mars   B. Uranus

    C. Saturn   D. Jupiter

18. The planet having mass, size and density close to Earth?

    A. Mars   B. Venus

    C. Saturn   D. Uranus

19. An astronaut in outer space will observe sky as ----

    A. White   B. Black

    C. Blue   D. Red

20. Our solar system orbits around

    A. Starburst   B. Whirlpool

    C. IC 1101   D. Milky way

Quiz-40

1. In our solar system, the planets known as the giant planets are also known as the outer planets?

   A. True   B. False

2. As the comet gets closer to the Sun, what happens to the length of its tail?

   A. Decreases   B. Remain the same

   C. Increases   D. It dies

3. What causes the gas tail of a comet to always point away from the sun?

   A. Solar wind   B. Air pressure

   C. Centrifugal force   D. Gravity

4. The solar wind bombards the Earth at 400 km/s, but the --- of the Earth protects us.

   A. Gravity   B. Magnetic field

   C. Ozone layer   D. Troposphere layer

5. The fifth-largest moon in the solar system?

   A. Earth's Moon   B. Titan

   C. Callisto   D. Io

6. Which comet was visible to the naked eye in 1996-97?

   A. Comet Halley   B. Comet West

   C. Comet Shoemaker   D. Comet Hale-Bopp

7. Which moon of Saturn is half bright and half dark

   A. Titan   B. Ganymede

   C. Iapetus   D. Enceladus

8. Which of the following objects orbit around Sun?

 A. Asteroid B. Comets

 C. Planets D. All of the above

9. Which planets are never visible at midnight?

 A. Neptune and Uranus B. Mercury and Venus

 C. Pluto and Saturn D. Jupiter and Saturn

10. Which of the following planets are called as Gas giants

 A. Jupiter and Neptune B. Saturn and Earth

 C. Jupiter and Saturn D. Neptune and Jupiter

11. Which part of the Sun is visible by a human?

 A. Photosphere B. Core

 C. Corona D. Chromosphere

12. Which of the following planets is a terrestrial planet?

 A. Saturn B. Jupiter

 C. Mars D. Neptune

13. The wrong statements about terrestrial planets?

 A. Made of rocky material B. Surfaces are solid

 C. They have rings D. A and B

14. Stars are hot bodies of gases composed of ----

 A. Oxygen and Nitrogen B. Hydrogen and Helium

 C. Hydrogen and oxygen D. Carbon-di-oxide

15. Saturn, Uranus, Neptune, Jupiter are ---- Planets?

 A. Jovian B. Terrestrial

 C. Rocky D. Inner

16. One of the moons of Jupiter?

    A. Titan   B. Triton

    C. Io   D. Eris

17. Nearest star from Earth?

    A. Sirius   B. Sun

    C. Proxima Centauri   D. Tau Ceti

18. Only planet known to have life?

    A. Earth   B. Venus

    C. Saturn   D. Mars

19. There is a red spot on this planet bigger than Earth?

    A. Jupiter   B. Neptune

    C. Saturn   D. Uranus

20. A planet is nearer to the Sun as compared to the Earth. Its distance from Sun is ---

    A. More than 1.0 AU   B. Less than 1.0 AU

    C. Equal to 1.00 AU   D. None of the above

Quiz-41

1. Distance of the farthest planet, Neptune from the Sun?

   A. 20 AU

   B. 30 AU

   C. 40 AU

   D. 50 AU

2. How many kilometers in 1 AU?

   A. 50,000,000 km

   B. 100,000,000 km

   C. 150,000,000 km

   D. 200,000,000 km

3. Which planet has the biggest moon in solar system?

   A. Jupiter

   B. Saturn

   C. Uranus

   D. Earth

4. The smallest moon in our solar system?

   A. Deimos

   B. Earth's moon

   C. Phoebus

   D. Triton

5. The first Trans-Neptunian Objects (TNO) discovered ----

   A. Makemake

   B. Pluto

   C. Haumea

   D. Ceres

6. What is the Latin name for Sun?

   A. Hot

   B. Sol

   C. Fireball

   D. Surya

7. The planet having highest orbital eccentricity?

   A. Venus

   B. Saturn

   C. Mercury

   D. Mars

8. The wind can blow at supersonic speeds on this planet?

   A   Neptune   B.   Venus

   C.   Saturn   D.   Mars

9. Which of the following planets spins backward?

   A.   Venus   B.   Neptune

   C.   Mars   D.   Mercury

10. Which celestial body in the solar system is considered almost a perfect sphere ever observed in nature?

   A.   Mercury   B.   Pluto

   C.   Sun   D.   Haumea

11. Your weight will be minimum on which planet?

   A.   Venus   B.   Neptune

   C.   Jupiter   D.   Mars

12. The Sun accounts for how much percentage of the weight of the total solar system?

   A.   10.08%   B.   48.36%

   C.   89.22%   D.   99.86%

13. The Kuiper belt lies between ----

   A.   Mars and Jupiter   B.   Saturn and Uranus

   C.   Beyond Neptune   D.   Nearest to Sun

14. The inner and outer Solar Systems are separated by

   A.   The scattered disc   B.   The asteroid belt

   C.   The Oort clouds   D.   The Kuiper belt

15. Eris, Haumea, and Makemake are examples of ----

    A. Moons
    B. Comets
    C. Dwarf planets
    D. Meteorites

16. What is the age of our solar system?

    A. 2.8 billion years
    B. 4.6 billion years
    C. 6.4 billion years
    D. 12 billion years

17. The dwarf planets Pluto, Makemake, Haumea are also known as

    A. Trans-Neptunian Objects
    B. Ice Objects
    C. Gas Objects
    D. Terrestrial objects

18. Uranus and Neptune together are referred to as the

    A. Terrestrial planets
    B. Gas giants
    C. Ice giants
    D. Outer giants

19. What is home to the known dwarf planets Pluto, Haumea and Makemake

    A. Kuiper belt
    B. Asteroid belt
    C. Oort clouds
    D. Inner belt

20. An extended shell of icy objects that exist in the outermost reaches of the solar system is called ---

    A. Kuiper belt
    B. Asteroid belt
    C. Oort clouds
    D. Outer belt

Quiz-42

1. Identify this planet? The winds on this planet can blow at supersonic speeds

   A. Uranus
   B. Saturn
   C. Neptune
   D. Titan

2. Identify this planet? This is the 7th planet from the Sun

   A. Uranus
   B. Mars
   C. Jupiter
   D. Neptune

167

3. Which is this moon? The surface of this is heavily cratered than any other moon in our solar system

   A. Triton
   B. Io
   C. Callisto
   D. Titan

4. Name this dwarf planet? Before 2006, this was the ninth planet of our solar system.

   A. Triton
   B. Titan
   C. Pluto
   D. Charon

5. Name this dwarf planet? It is the second-brightest object in the Kuiper Belt as seen from Earth

A. Mars
B. Makemake
C. Titan
D. Haumea

6. Identify this dwarf planet, which is least circular of all dwarf planets?

A. Haumea
B. Triton
C. Eris
D. Makemake

7. Name this dwarf planet found in the asteroid belt?

   A. Titan
   B. Haumea
   C. Ceres
   D. Triton

8. Identify this dwarf planet, the second-largest known dwarf planet in the Solar System?

   A. Io
   B. Titan
   C. Triton
   D. Eris

9. Identify this moon, the largest in the solar system?

    A. Ganymede
    B. Triton
    C. Makemake
    D. Titan

10. Name this moon of Saturn, the second-largest in the solar system?

    A. Triton
    B. Eris
    C. Ganemede
    D. Titan

11. Identify this moon of Neptune, which orbits in the opposite direction of its planet's rotation?

   A. Triton
   B. Io
   C. Titan
   D. Haumea

12. Name this "periodic" comet which returns to Earth's vicinity about every 75 years

   A. Neowise
   B. Hale Bopp
   C. Halley's Comet
   D. None of the above

13. The following symbol represents which planet?

   A. The Earth
   B. Saturn
   C. Venus
   D. Mars

14. Which planet is represented by this symbol?

   A. Jupiter
   B. Mars
   C. Neptune
   D. Mercury

15. This symbol represents which planet?

   A. Jupiter
   B. Neptune
   C. Mercury
   D. Saturn

16. The following symbol represents which planet?

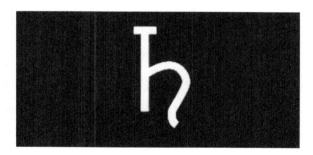

   A. Saturn
   B. Uranus
   C. Mercury
   D. Saturn

174

17. The following symbol represents which planet?

   A. Pluto
   B. Uranus
   C. Neptune
   D. Jupiter

18. This symbol represents which planet?

   A. Earth
   B. Venus
   C. Uranus
   D. Mercury

19. Which planet is represented by this symbol?

   A. Saturn
   B. Neptune
   C. Mercury
   D. Jupiter

20. Which planet is represented by this symbol?

   A. Mars
   B. The Earth
   C. Neptune
   D. Uranus

Quiz-43

The sizes of four terrestrial planets are compared below. Answer the following questions

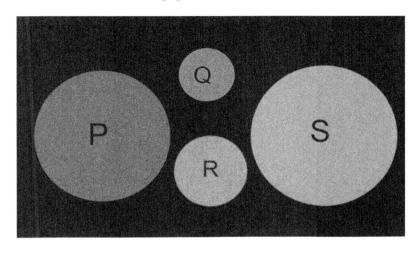

1. Identify the planet the Earth?

   A. 'P'   B. 'Q'

   B. 'R'   D. 'S'

2. Which planet is Mercury?

   A. 'P'   B. 'Q'

   B. 'R'   D. 'S'

3. Identify the planet Mars?

   A. 'P'   B. 'Q'

   B. 'R'   D. 'S'

The sizes of four terrestrial planets are compared below. Answer the following questions

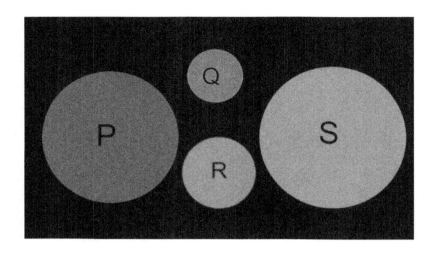

4. Identify the planet Venus?
   A. 'P'   B. 'Q'
   B. 'R'   D. 'S'

5. Which planet is nearest to the Sun?
   A. 'P'   B. 'Q'
   B. 'R'   D. 'S'

6. Which planet is furthest from the Sun?
   A. 'P'   B. 'Q'
   B. 'R'   D. 'S'

The sizes of four gas giants are compared below. Answer the following questions

7. Identify the planet Neptune?

   A. 'P'   B. 'Q'
   B. 'R'   D. 'S'

8. Which planet is Saturn?

   A. 'P'   B. 'Q'
   B. 'R'   D. 'S'

9. Which planet is nearest to the Sun?

   A. 'P'   B. 'Q'
   B. 'R'   D. 'S'

The sizes of four gas giants are compared below. Answer the following questions

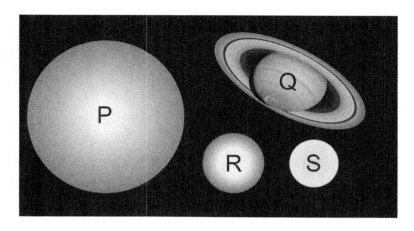

10. Identify the planet Jupiter?

    A. 'P'   B. 'Q'
    B. 'R'   D. 'S'

11. Which planet is Uranus?

    A. 'P'   B. 'Q'
    B. 'R'   D. 'S'

12. Which planet is furthest from the Sun?

    A. 'P'   B. 'Q'
    B. 'R'   D. 'S'

Eight planets of our solar system are shown in order from the Sun. Sizes are intentionally not shown to the scale. Identify these planets?

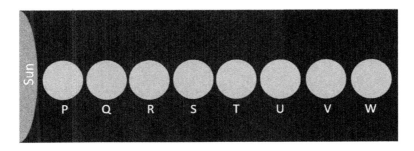

13. Identify the planet 'P'?

    A. Saturn   B. The Earth
    C. Jupiter   D. Mercury

14. Which planet is Neptune?

    A. 'R'   B. 'U'
    B. 'W'   D. 'T'

15. Identify the planet 'S'?

    A. Saturn   B. Mars
    C. Uranus   D. Mercury

Eight planets of our solar system are shown in order from the Sun. Sizes are intentionally not shown to the scale. Identify these planets?

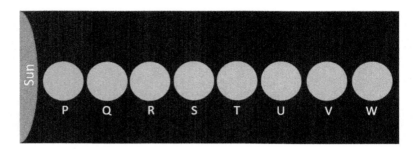

16. Which is the planet 'R'?

    A. Saturn   B. The Earth

    C. Jupiter   D. Neptune

17. Which planet is Jupiter?

    A. 'Q'   B. 'R'

    B. 'S'   D. 'T'

18. Identify the planet Uranus?

    A. 'P'   B. 'Q'

    C. 'V'   D. 'W'

Eight planets of our solar system are shown in order from the Sun. Sizes are intentionally not shown to the scale. Identify these planets?

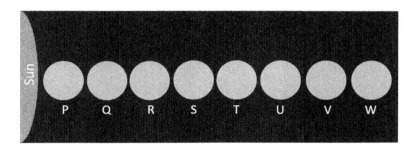

19 Identify the planet Saturn?

   A. 'R'
   B. 'T'
   C. 'U'
   D. 'W'

20. Which planet is Venus?

   A. 'P'
   B. 'Q'
   C. 'R'
   D. 'W'

25. Your weight & Age on Planets

Quiz-44

1. If your weight is 100 kg on Earth, then what is your weight on Mercury?

   A. 38 kg

   B. 52 kg

   C. 76 kg

   D. 100 kg

2. If your weight is 100 kg on Earth, then what is your weight on Venus?

   A. 50 kg

   B. 78 kg

   C. 91kg

   D. 100 kg

3. If your weight is 100 kg on Earth, then what is your weight on Jupiter?

   A. 100 kg

   B. 236 kg

   C. 288 kg

   D. 308 kg

4. If your mass is 100 kg on Earth, then your mass on Moon is ---

   A. 100 kg

   B. 166.6 kg

   C. 6.66 kg

   D. 16.66 kg

5. If your weight is 100 kg on Earth, then what is your weight on Mars?

   A. 18 kg

   B. 38 kg

   C. 52 kg

   D. 72 kg

6. If your weight is 100 kg on Earth, then what is your weight on Saturn?

   A. 68 kg

   B. 91 kg

   C. 100 kg

   D. 121 kg

7. If you weigh 100 kg on Earth, your weight on Uranus?

   A. 48 kg   B. 67 kg

   C. 89 kg   D. 121 kg

8. If your weight is 100 kg on Earth, then what is your weight on Neptune?

   A. 51 kg   B. 77 kg

   C. 100 kg   D. 112 kg

9. If your weight is 10 kg on Moon, your weight on Earth?

   A. 40 kg   B. 50 kg

   C. 60 kg   D. 70 kg

10. Considering all planets, your weight will be minimum on Mars

   A. True   B. False

11. If your age is 10 years on Earth, then what is your age on Mercury?

   A. 10 years   B. 28 years

   C. 42 years   D. 88 years

12. If your age is 10 years on Earth, then what is your age on Mars?

   A. 1.2 years   B. 5.3 years

   C. 10 years   D. 18.6 years

13. If your age is 10 years on Earth, then what is your age on Saturn?

   A. 0.34 years   B. 1 years

   C. 12 years   D. 21 years

14. If your age is 10 years on Earth, then your age on Venus?

    A. 10 years   B. 16 years

    C. 32 years   D. 48 years

15. If your age is 10 years on Earth, your age on Uranus?

    A. 0.12 years   B. 1.8 years

    C. 5.6 years   D. 10.5 years

16. If your age is 10 years on Earth, your age on Neptune?

    A. 0.01 years   B. 0.061 years

    C. 1.8 years   D. 4.3 years

17. If your age is 10 years on Earth, your age on Jupiter?

    A. 0.22 years   B. 0.84 years

    C. 1.64 years   D. 4.24 years

18. If your age is 10 years on Earth, then what is your age on Moon?

    A. 10 years   B. 46 years

    C. 92 years   D. 135 years

19. Compared to Earth, your age will be minimum on which planet

    A. Neptune   B. Mars

    C. Saturn   D. Uranus

20. Compared to Earth, your age will be maximum on which planet

    A. Neptune   B. Jupiter

    C. Mercury   D. Saturn

26. Famous Astronomers

Quiz-45

1. Who is considered as Father of Astronomy?

   A. Carl Sagan
   B. Nicolaus Copernicus
   C. Claudius Ptolemy
   D. Albert Einstein

2. Who described the geocentric theory which placed the Earth at the center of the solar system?

   A. Johannes Kepler
   B. Galileo Galilei
   C. Claudius Ptolemy
   D. Christiaan Huygens

3. Who proposed the heliocentric (sun-centered) model?

   A. Charles Messier
   B. Nicolaus Copernicus
   C. Claudius Ptolemy
   D. Albert Einstein

4. Who told that the planets do not travel in perfect circles around the Sun, but rather move in elliptical orbits?

   A. Claudius Ptolemy
   B. Johannes Kepler
   C. Galileo Galilei
   D. Isaac Newton

5. Which astronomer discovered the Galilean moons?

   A. Johannes Kepler
   A. Isaac Newton
   C. Christiaan Huygens
   C. Galileo Galilei

6. Who gave the famous three laws of planetary motion?

   A. Isaac Newton
   B. Galileo Galilei
   C. Claudius Ptolemy
   D. Johannes Kepler

7. Who proposed that a thin, flat ring circled Saturn

   A. Galileo Galilei
   B. Charles Messier
   C. Christiaan Huygens
   D. Giovanni Cassini

8. Who discovered the Cassini Division in the rings of Saturn in 1675?

    A. Christiaan Huygens   B. Giovanni Cassini

    C. Charles Cassini   D. Cassini Steve

9. Theory of relativity was proposed by?

    A. Giovanni Cassini   B. Charles Messier

    C. Albert Einstein   D. Carl Sagan

10. Who discovered the high temperatures of Venus and the seasonal changes on Mars?

    A. Giovanni Cassini   B. Charles Messier

    C. Albert Einstein   D. Carl Sagan

11. What was the name of the popular television show by famous astronomer, Carl Sagan?

    A. Astronomy   B. Cosmos

    C. Universe   D. Space Mysteries

12. The universal law of gravitation was proposed by?

    A. Isaac Newton   A. Christiaan Huygens

    C. Albert Einstein   C. Charles Messier

13. A Brief History of Time was written by?

    A. Giovanni Cassini   B. Charles Messier

    C. Albert Einstein   D. Stephen Hawking

14. Who discovered Uranus?

    A. Charles Messier   B. Albert Einstein

    C. Carl Sagan   D. William Herschel

15. Who discovered the largest asteroid, Ceres?

    A. Carl Sagan   B. William Herschel
    C. Giuseppe Piazzi   D. Charles Messier

16. Who was the first to observe the moons of Jupiter and the rings of Saturn with a telescope?

    A. Galileo Galilei   B. Isaac Newton
    C. Johannes Kepler   D. Christiaan Huygens

17. Who discovered the 76-year cycle comet that bears his name?

    A. Charles Messier   B. Edmond Halley
    C. William Herschel   D. Giovanni Cassini

18. Who discovered the existence of galaxies outside our own Milky Way galaxy?

    A. Carl Sagan   B. Edwin Hubble
    C. William Herschel   D. Giuseppe Piazzi

19. Which woman astronomer is credited with the discoveries of several comets?

    A. Carl Sagan   A. William Herschel
    C. Caroline Herschel   C. Christiaan Huygens

20. Who discovered Pluto in 1930?

    A. Giovanni Cassini   B. Clyde William Tombaugh
    C. Johannes Kepler   D. Carl Sagan

Quiz-46

1. Who discovered Andromeda Nebula?

   A. Stephen Hawking
   B. William Herschel
   C. Giuseppe Piazzi
   D. Edwin Hubble

2. Which astronomer is having a comet named after him?

   A. William Herschel
   B. Giuseppe Piazzi
   C. Edwin Hubble
   D. Edmund Halley

3. Who observed that the universe is expanding?

   A. Giuseppe Piazzi
   B. Edwin Hubble
   C. Giovanni Cassini
   D. Charles Messier

4. Which astronomer is famous for having space telescope named after him?

   A. Giuseppe Piazzi
   B. William Herschel
   C. Edwin Hubble
   D. Carl Sagan

5. Who discovered Neptune?

   A. Johann Gottfried Galle
   B. William Herschel
   C. Giuseppe Piazzi
   D. Carl Sagan

6. Which astronomer said that planets revolve around Sun in elliptical orbit and not in circular orbit?

   A. Johannes Kepler
   B. Giuseppe Piazzi
   C. William Herschel
   D. Carl Sagan

7. Who discovered four moons of Saturn?

   A. Stephen Hawking
   B. Giuseppe Piazzi
   C. William Herschel
   D. Giovanni Cassini

8. Who wrote the book "The Revolution of Celestial Orbs"

    A. Johannes Kepler   B. Isaac Newton

    C. Nicholas Copernicus   D. Claudius Ptolemy

9. Who was the first to discover the movement of sunspots?

    A. Galileo Galilei   B. Isaac Newton

    C. Johannes Kepler   D. Christiaan Huygens

10. Who discovered Pluto on January 1, 1801

    A. Galileo Galilei   B. Giuseppe Piazzi

    C. Christiaan Huygens   D. William Herschel

11. Who first predicted that the planets and the Moon shine by reflected sunlight?

    A. Aryabhata   B. Johannes Kepler

    C. Claudius Ptolemy   D. Galileo Galilei

12. Who proposed that the mass of a white dwarf can not exceed 1.44 times that of the Sun?

    A. S. Chandrasekhar   B. Charles Messier

    C. Christiaan Huygens   D. Aryabhata

13. The name of the book written by Claudius Ptolemy?

    A. Unexplored Universe   B. The Almagest

    C. Astronomica   D. Beyond Stars

14. Who first gave the value of π up to four digits?

    A. Bhaskara   B. Aryabhata

    C. Claudius Ptolemy   D. Galileo Galilei

15. Which famous book dealing with mathematics and astronomy was written by Aryabhata?

    A. Astrobhata   B. Antrikshgyan

    C. Aryabhatiya   D. Bhatasutras

16. Who put forth that the Earth had once been hit by a planet sized body, creating both the Moon and the Earth's 23.5° tilt?

    A. Christiaan Huygens   B. Giuseppe Piazzi

    C. William K. Hartmann   D. Albert Einstein

17. Who first gave the value of π up to four digits?

    A. Bhaskara   B. Aryabhata

    C. Claudius Ptolemy   D. Galileo Galilei

18. Who introduced the concept of zero?

    A. Bhaskara   B. Albert Einstein

    C. Aryabhata   D. Galileo Galilei

19. Comet Encke is named after which astronomer for his calculation of its orbit.

    A. Johann Franz Encke   B. Encke Robert

    C. Fredrick Lewis. Encke D. Christiaan Huygens

20. Who calculated the size of the Milky Way galaxy and general location of its center?

    A. Giuseppe Piazzi   B. Galileo Galilei

    C. William Herschel   D. Harlow Shapley

27. Crossword Puzzle in Astronomy
Quiz-47

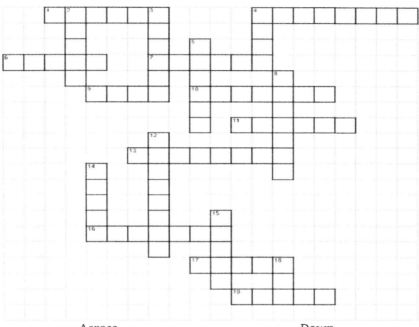

Across
1. Smallest moon in solar system
4. We live in this galaxy
6. Largest dwarf planet
7. The 7th planet from Sun
9. Earth's natural satellite
10. Planet nearest to the Sun
11. It is a retrograde moon
13. Biggest moon in the solar system
16. Farthest planet from the Sun
17. Smallest dwarf planet
19. Second brightest object in the night sky

Down
2. Densest planet in solar system
3. Has spectacular ring system
4. Also called red planet
5. Least circular dwarf planet
8. Largest planet in solar system
12. Most heavily cratered moon in solar system
14. Saturn's largest moon
15. Largest moon in solar system
18. Only star in our solar system

Quiz-48

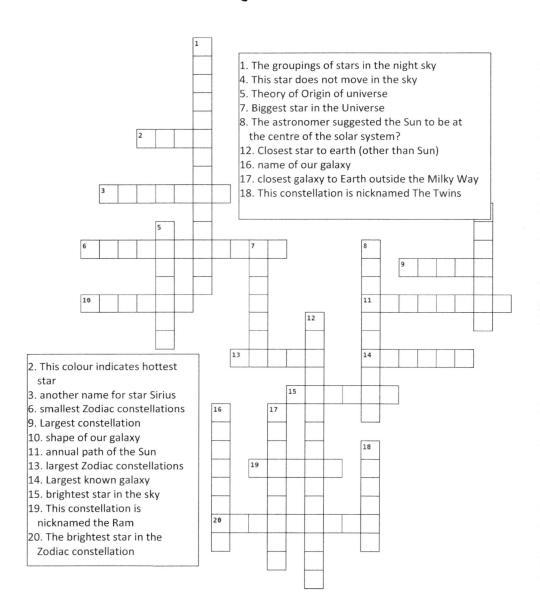

28. Search the word Puzzle in Astronomy

Quiz-49

A	C	V	C	O	M	E	T	W	R	F	G	A
M	U	E	O	A	S	T	E	R	I	S	M	N
P	K	U	N	I	V	E	R	S	E	L	R	D
I	S	S	S	S	I	R	I	U	S	C	T	R
C	A	S	T	E	R	O	I	D	D	U	U	O
1	Y	F	E	A	R	T	H	D	G	D	N	M
1	P	O	L	A	R	I	S	H	M	J	I	E
0	G	A	L	A	X	Y	K	G	N	T	H	D
1	F	R	A	S	T	R	O	N	O	M	Y	A
O	R	D	T	S	F	H	I	P	M	H	D	G
Y	S	M	I	L	K	Y	W	A	Y	F	R	F
O	A	M	O	H	U	B	B	L	E	S	A	D
P	L	A	N	E	T	O	K	V	I	R	G	O

29. Unscramble the letters in Astronomy

Quiz-50

1.	NUS	
2.	ARTS	
3.	TRONSOAMY	
4.	ROOT LOCUD	
5.	SERVIEUN	
6.	STONELLCATION	
7.	ROADAMEND	
8.	RISUIS	
9.	PERSUNOAV	
10.	11ICO	
11.	LBACK LEOH	
12.	BUBLEH	
13.	MOSCIC	
14.	TLIGH AREY	
15.	NARUL	
16.	RASOL	
17.	BULANE	
18.	PALENT	
19.	CAZOID	
20.	SUPLAR	

Quiz-51

1.	LASOR MESSYT	
2.	RUPJETI	
3.	NATURS	
4.	THEAR	
5.	RAMS	
6.	CURREMY	
7.	SURANU	
8.	TUNEPEN	
9.	TINTA	
10.	TOLUP	
11.	MONO	
12.	TECOM	
13.	AEROIDST	
14.	MEREOT	
15.	ROBIT	
16.	LAGAXY	
17.	MIYWALKY	
18.	MEDEANYG	
19.	SEPLICE	
20.	TOPNUSS	

30. Answers to all quizzes

Answers to Quiz-1							
1	B	6	A	11	A	16	B
2	D	7	A	12	D	17	C
3	B	8	A	13	B	18	C
4	A	9	B	14	C	19	C
5	C	10	B	15	B	20	C

Answers to Quiz-2							
1	B	6	D	11	A	16	A
2	C	7	A	12	D	17	C
3	D	8	B	13	B	18	A
4	C	9	B	14	D	19	B
5	A	10	D	15	B	20	D

Answers to Quiz-3							
1	C	6	D	11	B	16	D
2	B	7	C	12	B	17	C
3	C	8	B	13	A	18	D
4	A	9	B	14	B	19	C
5	A	10	C	15	D	20	A

Answers to Quiz-4							
1	C	6	D	11	A	16	B
2	A	7	C	12	B	17	C
3	B	8	B	13	B	18	C
4	D	9	C	14	D	19	C
5	C	10	B	15	A	20	B

Answers to Quiz-5							
1	C	6	B	11	C	16	C
2	B	7	A	12	B	17	D
3	D	8	A	13	C	18	B
4	A	9	D	14	A	19	A
5	D	10	B	15	D	20	C

Answers to Quiz-6							
1	B	6	D	11	B	16	A
2	D	7	C	12	C	17	D
3	A	8	A	13	B	18	C
4	C	9	C	14	A	19	A
5	B	10	D	15	C	20	B

Answers to Quiz-7							
1	A	6	C	11	B	16	A
2	B	7	B	12	C	17	A
3	C	8	C	13	C	18	D
4	B	9	C	14	B	19	C
5	D	10	A	15	B	20	A

Answers to Quiz-8							
1	A	6	B	11	B	16	C
2	A	7	C	12	D	17	C
3	B	8	C	13	A	18	B
4	A	9	D	14	D	19	A
5	D	10	A	15	A	20	B

Answers to Quiz-9							
1	B	6	C	11	B	16	C
2	D	7	A	12	B	17	A
3	C	8	C	13	A	18	A
4	B	9	A	14	C	19	D
5	A	10	C	15	D	20	B

Answers to Quiz-10							
1	B	6	C	11	C	16	D
2	B	7	C	12	C	17	D
3	A	8	B	13	A	18	A
4	C	9	C	14	D	19	C
5	D	10	B	15	B	20	C

Answers to Quiz-11							
1	D	6	C	11	D	16	D
2	B	7	A	12	C	17	D
3	A	8	C	13	D	18	C
4	C	9	A	14	A	19	A
5	A	10	C	15	D	20	A

Answers to Quiz-12							
1	B	6	B	11	B	16	C
2	A	7	D	12	B	17	B
3	A	8	D	13	A	18	B
4	C	9	A	14	B	19	D
5	B	10	A	15	D	20	C

Answers to Quiz-13							
1	B	6	B	11	D	16	A
2	A	7	C	12	B	17	C
3	B	8	D	13	A	18	D
4	C	9	B	14	C	19	C
5	B	10	A	15	D	20	C

Answers to Quiz-14							
1	B	6	A	11	C	16	C
2	B	7	A	12	B	17	B
3	A	8	D	13	C	18	B
4	C	9	A	14	C	19	C
5	B	10	A	15	D	20	D

Answers to Quiz-15							
1	D	6	B	11	B	16	D
2	D	7	A	12	C	17	C
3	B	8	D	13	A	18	D
4	A	9	C	14	D	19	A
5	B	10	C	15	C	20	B

Answers to Quiz-16							
1	A	6	D	11	C	16	B
2	C	7	A	12	C	17	A
3	C	8	D	13	A	18	B
4	B	9	A	14	A	19	C
5	C	10	A	15	B	20	A

Answers to Quiz-17							
1	A	6	C	11	D	16	C
2	A	7	B	12	D	17	A
3	B	8	D	13	A	18	B
4	A	9	A	14	B	19	A
5	C	10	A	15	C	20	D

Answers to Quiz-18							
1	D	6	B	11	C	16	A
2	B	7	C	12	B	17	A
3	C	8	C	13	A	18	B
4	A	9	B	14	B	19	A
5	D	10	B	15	C	20	B

Answers to Quiz-19							
1	B	6	B	11	C	16	A
2	A	7	C	12	A	17	B
3	C	8	B	13	B	18	B
4	B	9	D	14	C	19	D
5	A	10	D	15	C	20	B

Answers to Quiz-20							
1	A	6	B	11	B	16	A
2	A	7	D	12	A	17	C
3	C	8	B	13	B	18	D
4	B	9	A	14	C	19	C
5	C	10	B	15	D	20	A

Answers to Quiz-21							
1	C	6	B	11	D	16	B
2	B	7	A	12	C	17	A
3	D	8	A	13	A	18	A
4	A	9	B	14	C	19	C
5	B	10	B	15	B	20	B

Answers to Quiz-22							
1	C	6	C	11	A	16	C
2	A	7	B	12	D	17	C
3	B	8	C	13	C	18	B
4	D	9	C	14	D	19	B
5	A	10	A	15	B	20	C

Answers to Quiz-23							
1	C	6	A	11	A	16	D
2	B	7	B	12	B	17	A
3	C	8	C	13	B	18	C
4	D	9	D	14	C	19	A
5	A	10	A	15	C	20	D

Answers to Quiz-24							
1	D	6	A	11	B	16	B
2	C	7	A	12	A	17	C
3	C	8	C	13	B	18	B
4	A	9	A	14	C	19	A
5	A	10	A	15	D	20	D

Answers to Quiz-25							
1	D	6	B	11	B	16	D
2	C	7	A	12	C	17	C
3	B	8	D	13	B	18	B
4	A	9	B	14	A	19	B
5	C	10	A	15	C	20	A

Answers to Quiz-26							
1	B	6	C	11	D	16	C
2	C	7	B	12	C	17	D
3	C	8	B	13	B	18	A
4	A	9	D	14	D	19	B
5	B	10	A	15	A	20	A

Answers to Quiz-27							
1	C	6	C	11	A	16	D
2	B	7	B	12	D	17	B
3	C	8	B	13	D	18	A
4	C	9	A	14	C	19	C
5	B	10	A	15	D	20	C

Answers to Quiz-28							
1	C	6	D	11	D	16	C
2	A	7	C	12	B	17	D
3	B	8	A	13	A	18	C
4	B	9	C	14	C	19	A
5	B	10	D	15	A	20	A

Answers to Quiz-29							
1	B	6	B	11	D	16	A
2	B	7	C	12	B	17	C
3	D	8	C	13	A	18	A
4	A	9	A	14	C	19	D
5	A	10	A	15	D	20	B

Answers to Quiz-30							
1	C	6	C	11	C	16	B
2	B	7	A	12	C	17	C
3	B	8	A	13	B	18	C
4	D	9	C	14	C	19	B
5	C	10	A	15	D	20	D

Answers to Quiz-31							
1	A	6	C	11	C	16	A
2	C	7	A	12	A	17	B
3	A	8	D	13	C	18	D
4	B	9	C	14	C	19	D
5	A	10	A	15	D	20	C

Answers to Quiz-32							
1	D	6	B	11	C	16	D
2	A	7	C	12	A	17	D
3	D	8	B	13	C	18	A
4	A	9	A	14	A	19	A
5	A	10	A	15	D	20	A

Answers to Quiz-33							
1	A	6	C	11	A	16	A
2	B	7	A	12	A	17	B
3	C	8	B	13	B	18	A
4	A	9	D	14	C	19	C
5	C	10	A	15	A	20	D

Answers to Quiz-34							
1	B	6	B	11	C	16	A
2	C	7	B	12	B	17	B
3	A	8	A	13	D	18	C
4	B	9	A	14	D	19	A
5	B	10	A	15	C	20	B

Answers to Quiz-35							
1	C	6	B	11	A	16	A
2	A	7	D	12	B	17	B
3	A	8	A	13	C	18	A
4	A	9	B	14	C	19	C
5	A	10	A	15	A	20	A

Answers to Quiz-36							
1	C	6	B	11	C	16	B
2	B	7	A	12	B	17	B
3	A	8	D	13	A	18	A
4	A	9	B	14	C	19	D
5	D	10	B	15	C	20	A

Answers to Quiz-37							
1	B	6	A	11	D	16	D
2	C	7	D	12	B	17	B
3	A	8	C	13	A	18	D
4	B	9	C	14	A	19	D
5	B	10	A	15	A	20	C

Answers to Quiz-38							
1	D	6	D	11	D	16	D
2	A	7	B	12	B	17	D
3	D	8	A	13	A	18	B
4	C	9	B	14	C	19	B
5	B	10	C	15	C	20	D

Answers to Quiz-39							
1	B	6	A	11	C	16	C
2	C	7	C	12	B	17	B
3	C	8	A	13	D	18	A
4	A	9	B	14	A	19	B
5	A	10	B	15	D	20	D

Answers to Quiz-40							
1	A	6	D	11	A	16	C
2	C	7	C	12	C	17	B
3	A	8	D	13	C	18	A
4	B	9	B	14	B	19	A
5	A	10	C	15	A	20	B

Answers to Quiz-41							
1	B	6	B	11	D	16	B
2	C	7	C	12	D	17	A
3	A	8	A	13	C	18	C
4	A	9	A	14	B	19	A
5	B	10	C	15	C	20	C

Answers to Quiz-42							
1	C	6	A	11	A	16	A
2	A	7	C	12	C	17	B
3	C	8	D	13	C	18	A
4	C	9	A	14	D	19	D
5	B	10	D	15	B	20	A

Answers to Quiz-43							
1	D	6	C	11	C	16	B
2	B	7	D	12	D	17	D
3	C	8	B	13	D	18	C
4	A	9	A	14	C	19	C
5	B	10	A	15	B	20	B

Answers to Quiz-44							
1	A	6	B	11	C	16	B
2	C	7	C	12	B	17	B
3	B	8	D	13	A	18	D
4	A	9	C	14	B	19	A
5	B	10	A	15	A	20	C

Answers to Quiz-45							
1	B	6	D	11	B	16	A
2	C	7	C	12	A	17	B
3	B	8	B	13	D	18	B
4	B	9	C	14	D	19	C
5	C	10	D	15	C	20	B

Answers to Quiz-46							
1	D	6	A	11	A	16	C
2	D	7	D	12	A	17	B
3	B	8	C	13	B	18	C
4	C	9	A	14	B	19	A
5	A	10	B	15	C	20	D

Answer to Quiz-47

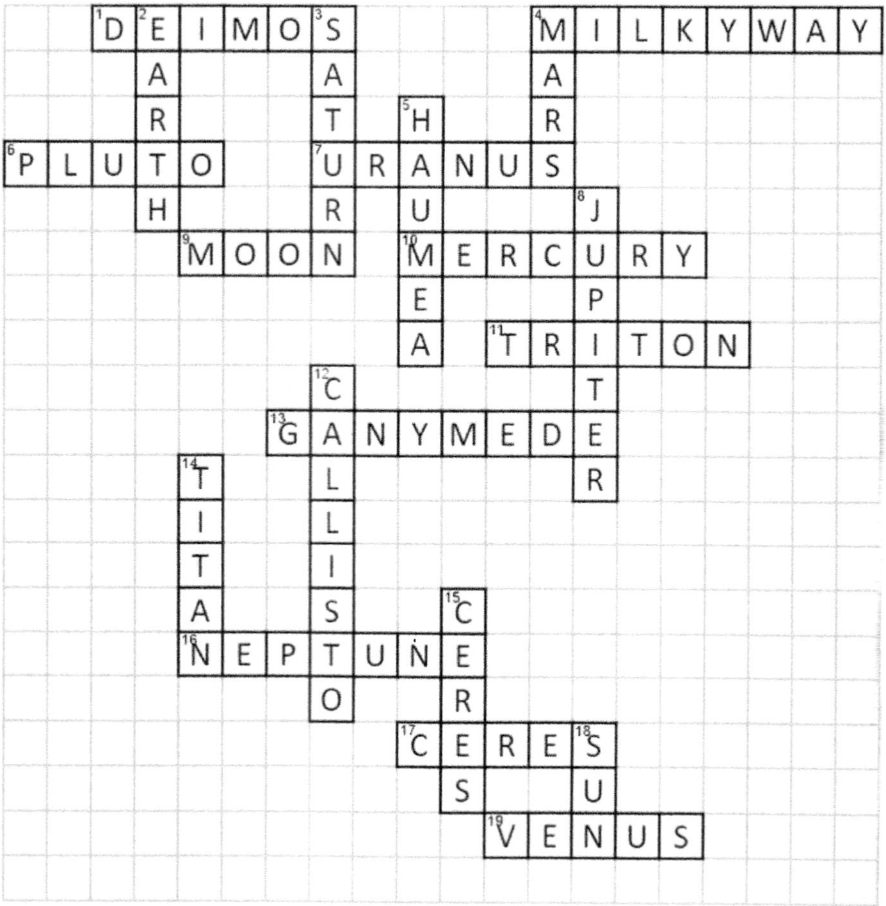
1 DEIMOS
2 EARTH
3 SATURN
4 MILKYWAY
4 MARS
5 HAUMEA
6 PLUTO
7 URANUS
8 JUPITER
9 MOON
10 MERCURY
11 TRITON
12 CALLISTO
13 GANYMEDE
14 TITAN
15 CERES
16 NEPTUNE
17 CERES
18 SUN
19 VENUS

Answers to Quiz-48

Answers to Quiz-49

A	C	V	C	O	M	E	T	W	R	F	G	A
M	U	E	O	A	S	T	E	R	I	S	M	N
P	K	U	N	I	V	E	R	S	E	L	R	D
I	S	S	S	S	I	R	I	U	S	C	T	R
C	A	S	T	E	R	O	I	D	D	U	U	O
1	Y	F	E	A	R	T	H	D	G	D	N	M
1	P	O	L	A	R	I	S	H	M	J	I	E
0	G	A	L	A	X	Y	K	G	N	T	H	D
1	F	R	A	S	T	R	O	N	O	M	Y	A
O	R	D	T	S	F	H	I	P	M	H	D	G
Y	S	M	I	L	K	Y	W	A	Y	F	R	F
O	A	M	O	H	U	B	B	L	E	S	A	D
P	L	A	N	E	T	O	K	V	I	R	G	O

214

Answer to Quiz-50

1.	NUS	SUN
2.	ARTS	STAR
3.	TRONSOAMY	ASTRONOMY
4.	ROOT LOCUD	OORT CLOUD
5.	SERVIEUN	UNIVERSE
6.	STONELLCATION	CONSTELLATION
7.	ROADAMEND	ANDROMEDA
8.	RISUIS	SIRIUS
9.	PERSUNOAV	SUPERNOVA
10.	11ICO	ICO11
11.	LBACK LEOH	BLACK HOLE
12.	BUBLEH	HUBBLE
13.	MOSCIC	COSMIC
14.	TLIGH AREY	LIGHT YEAR
15.	NARUL	LUNAR
16.	RASOL	SOLAR
17.	BULANE	NEBULA
18.	PALENT	PLANET
19.	CAZOID	ZODIAC
20.	SUPLAR	PULSAR

Answer to Quiz-51

1.	LASOR MESSYT	SOLAR SYSTEM
2.	RUPJETI	JUPITER
3.	NATURS	SATURN
4.	THEAR	EARTH
5.	RAMS	MARS
6.	CURREMY	MERCURY
7.	SURANU	URANUS
8.	TUNEPEN	NEPTUNE
9.	TINTA	TITAN
10.	TOLUP	PLUTO
11.	MONO	MOON
12.	TECOM	COMET
13.	AEROIDST	ASTEROID
14.	MEREOT	METEOR
15.	ROBIT	ORBIT
16.	LAGAXY	GALAXY
17.	MIYWALKY	MILKYWAY
18.	MEDEANYG	GANYMEDE

31. Disclaimer

The questions and answers given here have been designed from wide reputable resources. While reasonable care has been taken in providing correct information here, the author will not be responsible for the accuracy of the data given here. It is strongly recommended that information given here be checked against other sources before actual use. The author will not be held liable for any direct, indirect, consequential or incidental damages incurred through. Please send your comments, suggestions and mistakes, if any for implementation in the next version of this document.

Dr RK Sharma

e-mail: rks.aesi@gmail.com